London
for
Families

London
for
Families

by Larry Lain
and Michael Lain

INTERLINK BOOKS

An imprint of Interlink Publishing Group, Inc.
New York

First published in 1998 by

INTERLINK BOOKS
An imprint of Interlink Publishing Group, Inc.
99 Seventh Avenue
Brooklyn, New York 11215

Library of Congress Cataloging-in-Publication Data

Lain, Larry, 1947–
   London for families / by Larry Lain and Michael Lain.
     p. cm.
   Includes index.
   ISBN 1–56656–267–8
   1. Family recreation—England—London—Guidebooks. 2. London
(England)—Guidebooks. I. Lain, Michael. II. Title.
DA679.L24 1998   97–29647
914.21049859—dc21   CIP

Printed and bound in Canada
10 9 8 7 6 5 4 3 2 1

For the latest updates to *London for Families*,
check our page on the World Wide Web at

http://www.as.udayton.edu/com/faculty/lain/lonfam.htm

Contents

Part III: Planning Pages

Acknowledgments

No one ever really travels alone. Even those who buy a ticket for one have picked up ideas about destinations, things to see and do, and so on from other journeyers. Writing a book is much the same. Ideas and encouragement come from all directions, and we'd like to recognize the most important sources.

Not surprisingly, we would like most of all to acknowledge the help and support of our family, each member of which contributed ideas, advice, encouragement, and sometimes even copy to the book. So our greatest debt is owed to Barbara Lain, wife of Larry and mother of Mike; to the other Lain brothers Rik and Doug; and to Mike's wife Beth, who is now preparing for her first trip to London. These are the best imaginable travelling companions, whether it's through England or through life.

Our favorite travel agent, Rachel Sammons of AAA Travel in Beavercreek, Ohio, has saved us many headaches and much money over the years, and has been generous with her experience and advice throughout this project. The travel advice of colleagues and fellow Anglophiles Jeff Griffin and Jack Rang turns up throughout the book.

Finally, the suggestions, stories and experiences of individuals and families we have talked with, both at home and abroad, have provided ideas and insights and depth that will help ensure that *your* family will enjoy its trip as much as theirs did.

Introduction

H ello! You've bought our book. Or maybe you've borrowed it from the library or are browsing through it in a bookstore. In any case: Welcome! Apparently you were intrigued enough by the title to pick it up. That's the first step in the most fabulous family vacation you've ever had. No matter how far out it seems, the idea of taking your family to London has at least crossed your mind. In the chapters that follow, we're going to show you why it's easier than you thought and we'll give you the information you need to have a terrific time while you're there.

Why Go Abroad?

Why might you consider going to England instead of somewhere closer to home? If it's an idea that's even entered your mind, you're probably already interested in the history, the literature, the cultural background we share with the people of that country. Britain is a foreign country, but one enough like us to be manageable, different but not intimidating because of an incomprehensible language that limits our access.

Travel, especially to a foreign country, creates a unique bond among family members who are discovering and sharing new and exciting things every day and who are learning together to cope with an entirely new and different place. Foreign travel is a marvellous thing to offer to young people. The world is shrinking at a pace their parents could never have imagined: young people must be more world-oriented than their parents to live in the new century, and will need a greater understanding of other cultures than previous generations needed.

A trip abroad also leads children to a better understanding and appreciation of their own culture. It's illuminating to see the ways *other* people do things—not that they do them better or worse . . . just *differently*. It's not surprising that an experience like this often helps kids in school in subjects like literature, history, and other social studies, by giving them experiences and perspectives they could get in no other way.

This sort of trip isn't for everyone, though. Children less than ten years old will certainly get less from it than older children. Their understanding of their own culture is too limited to make many comparisons worthwhile, and they've had much less exposure to the history and literature that will create so many associations for them abroad. They'll remember less of the trip in future years than older children will, too. Our suggestions in this book, then, make little provision for very young children.

What About the Cost?

Vacations can be expensive wherever you go, but staying in the United States, or even in your home state, is no guarantee of having a cheap trip. *Uninformed* travel *anywhere* is terribly expensive, whether you're going to England, Disneyworld, or the state fair. But *informed* planning and travel can make almost any trip affordable. Airfare (which Chapter 3 will help with) is the most expensive part of a trip abroad. Once you're there, you can manage nicely on no more money than you might if you'd stayed home. In fact, we've found repeatedly that finding ways to save money adds to the pleasure of the vacation, because our experience is geared to *living like a local* . . . even as a tourist. That's the key, not only to an economical vacation, but to one rich in memorable experiences.

We get the most out of our travels when we become as much as possible *a part of* London, not when, like other tourists, we remain *apart from* the daily life of the city. That's why we recommend staying in an apartment, not a hotel, shopping where the locals shop, living the life of a Londoner whenever possible.

Taking a family abroad *can* be an expensive proposition, but it needn't empty your bank account if you plan ahead, know what to expect, and understand how to live as much within your means abroad as you do at home.

How This Book Can Help

That's what *London for Families* is all about: helping you find the best airfare and lodgings, and helping you find things to see and do that will be the most fun for your family. There are scores of London travel guides, but this one is unique because there is a real emphasis on family travel here, as well as a real concern with economy. We don't want to be all things to all people; the single traveller or the expense account traveller might find an idea or two in these pages, but that's only coincidental. We're interested in your family, because family trips *anywhere* have been the best trips we've taken, and going to London has been the best of the best.

We'll tell you about the don't-miss places that should be part of any trip to London, but we'll also help you find lesser-known attractions of particular interest to kids. We'll try to give you an idea of what a family can do with realistic one- to three-week itineraries. We'll stress the idea of getting the most for everyone from your trip by, as much a tourist can, *living like a local*, and perhaps most of all, talking often about how *staying flexible* can lead to a relaxed, fulfilling vacation for everyone, one that actually relieves more stress than it creates!

We hope perusing this book is more than just an interesting diversion for you; we hope it leads to the same kind of experience for your family that ours has had—a chance to create wonderful memories and a renewed family bond with the vacation of a lifetime, a trip to London. Come with us, now, as we help you plan your trip and then show you around one of our very favorite places. May your family enjoy it as much as ours has!

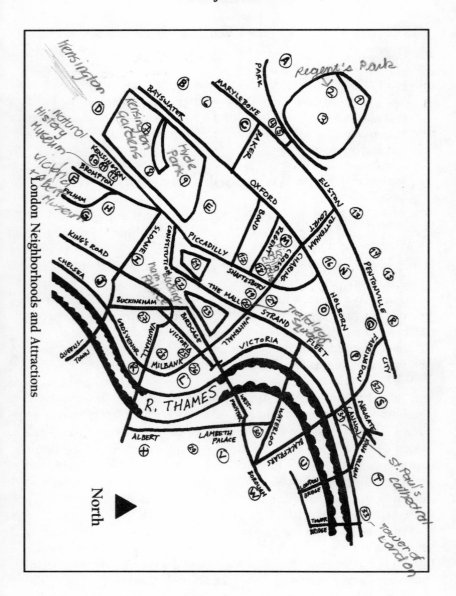

North

Map Key

Places of Interest		*Neighborhoods*	
1	Zoo	A	St. John's Wood
2	Regent's Park	B	Bayswater
3	Open Air Theatre	C	Marylebone
4	Madame Tussaud's	D	Kensington
5	Planetarium	E	Mayfair
6	Paddington Station	F	Earl's Court
7	Kensington Gardens	G	South Kensington
8	Serpentine	H	Brompton
9	Hyde Park	I	Belgravia
10	Science Museum	J	Chelsea
11	Natural History Museum	K	Pimlico
12	Victoria & Albert Museum	L	Westminster
13	Euston Station	M	Soho
14	St. Pancras Station	N	Bloomsbury
15	King's Cross Station	O	Holborn
16	British Museum & Library	P	The City
17	Museum of Mankind	Q	Clerkenwell
18	Piccadilly Circus	R	Islington
19	National Gallery	S	Barbican
20	Trafalgar Square	T	Spitalfields
21	Green Park	U	Southwark
22	Buckingham Palace	V	Lambeth
23	St. James's Park	W	Elephant & Castle
24	Covent Garden	X	Vauxhall
25	Westminster Abbey		
26	Houses of Parliament		
27	Victoria Station		
28	Tate Gallery		
29	Imperial War Museum		
30	Waterloo Station		
31	St. Paul's Cathedral		
32	Barbican Center		
33	Tower of London		

Part I:
The Basics

I n Part I we will focus on survival skills: basic planning, finding transportation, shelter, and food—and how to adjust to your temporary home once you arrive. We'll talk about creating a sense of excitement and adventure in your family, and provide lots of tips for getting the most out of your trip. The advice is practical, time-tested, and designed to provide a foolproof and stress-free guide even for someone who has never been out of the country before.

In these days of rapid transportation, even between continents, it may no longer be true that "getting there is half the fun," but we believe that *planning* a trip is, indeed, much of the fun of a vacation. Part I is dedicated to planning and to teaching you our philosophy of *living like a local*.

1. Planning Is the Key

A good family vacation, especially one to somewhere you've never been before, starts months before you leave home. For us the planning, the anticipation, the talking about things we want to do and see is one of the best parts of the trip. By the time we're ready to go we're excited by the prospect of the new things we'll discover, and already know enough about our destination to give us confidence that we can thrive even on the unexpected.

Before a trip we haunt bookstores and libraries, looking for books and magazine articles on the places we're heading, and keep a little notebook to jot down the most useful pieces of information we spot. We consider carefully all the advice we glean from books and magazines, from videos and computer discussion groups, from other people who have been where we're going. We *consider* it. And then we plan our own trip.

Some things *need* to be planned in advance if your family is to have a stress-free fun trip. Trust us: You do *not* want to show up with a family of five in a popular tourist destination at the height of the travel season without lodging arrangements! You'll probably find somewhere to stay, all right, but you may not be able to afford to leave your room to see anything! Don't run the risk of having to take the last room available in town—the one right above the 24-hour biker bar.

It's deadly, though, to try to plan every aspect of your trip. A vacation with too tight a schedule is one which will leave people exhausted and grouchy at the end of each day. You need room to be spontaneous, to be surprised. In this chapter we'll give you an overview of what kinds of things to plan ahead, and in the chapters that follow, we'll show you how.

When to Go, How Long to Stay

If you're travelling with a family, the *when* is largely dictated by the school calendar. The *ideal* time to travel is probably in the spring or fall, when the weather is mild and the crowds are at home, and when some prices are lower. That, alas, is seldom practical for an American family.

One off-season possibility is spring break, if your children have one. England isn't a warm-weather destination like Orlando; the weather can be rainy and cool. But we've been in England in both March and April and had delightful weather each time, with warm temperatures and sunny skies. The English weather is changeable; you're just as likely to hit glorious weather off season as you are to find drizzle.

If everyone can be free during the same week at spring break time, airfares and lodging rates will probably be lower, restaurants less crowded, and lines at attractions shorter. On the other hand, museums often have shorter hours during the off-season, and there are fewer of the colorful festivals and pageants that can be so much fun.

Most people have to go during the summer, however. That's OK too, but you'll want to plan a little further ahead to get the flights and accommodations you want.

If at all possible, make your summer trip in June, as soon as possible after the kids get out of school. There are several reasons for this:

- Most schools in Europe are in session until about July 1. London is a popular destination for French, German, and Italian families too, but they probably won't arrive until July or August. The city gets more crowded then.
- The weather is ideal for sightseeing. It gets light earlier and stays light later than it will later in the summer, and the days are usually warm and dry.
- Attractions are operating on their summer schedules by June, giving you more flexibility in deciding where to visit.
- Some of the most colorful local events take place in June.

For a family trip, try to spend at least seven days in London. Shorter trips are possible, because London is just six hours away from the East Coast. But shorter trips are exhausting and provide little chance for the growth of the family memories that have been the best part of our travels. This should be a trip to savor.

Tip: The pageantry of "Trooping the Colour" (see Chapter 11) is in mid-June. This spectacle is well worth seeing for the colorfully-dressed soldiers and horses and the stirring music of the military bands. On the other hand, other attractions, like the Tower of London, are much less crowded that day because so many people are at the "big" event. That could be an ideal day to be somewhere else. (And because it's a state holiday, the guards at the Tower will be wearing their colorful 16th-century uniforms, which make for great photographs.)

Spending less than a week can also raise the cost of airfare, because the best discounts are normally available for stays of between seven and thirty days. If you must make a shorter trip, try to do it during the off-season when airfares are lower. Chapter 3 covers these points in more detail.

A longer stay is also better because you won't be as tempted to try to pack *too* much into each day. On a trip like this, pacing is very important. Doing too much too soon can make everybody cranky. The sample itineraries in Chapter 19 provide a realistic look at what can be done in a day or a week. Unless you stay for a year you can't see and do everything, so don't try.

Budget Basics

We suggest that you consider two categories of expenditures, airfare and daily expenses. They are independent of each other and need to be approached in different ways.

The most expensive part of your trip to London will be getting there. Once you're there your trip should cost no more than a vacation at home, and can actually cost less. Remember: seven million people live in London. Very few of them are rich. If the British middle class can thrive there, so can you!

Airfare

Chapter 3 will give you some suggestions for finding the most economical airfare to London, but we'll make a few general points now.

First, rates are often much lower in the off-season, and this makes a spring or autumn trip more affordable, if everyone can get a break from work and school at the same time. But rates are volatile at all times of the year. Sales come and go without warning, and if there are 300 people on a transatlantic flight, they have probably paid at least a hundred different fares among them; this is a fact of air travel. If you begin your planning early and work with a travel agent who can help you keep an eye open for sales, and who can coach you in some creative approaches to finding a flight, you can do better than most people on the plane you take to London.

Living and Sightseeing Expenses

Now let's outline the rest of your budget.

Here are the other things you'll need to take into account when budgeting your trip. They are the same things you'd need to consider if you were going on vacation to Disneyworld, to Yellowstone, or to anywhere else.

- accommodations
- food
- attractions and sightseeing
- shopping
- local transportation

The best approach for this sort of vacation is to budget expenses on a per person/per day basis. That allows easy comparison of different sorts of lodging and allows for meals and admissions to be calculated easily. Here are some realistic figures. Note that when this book went to press, the British pound was valued at about $1.60 in U.S. currency. When we discuss prices in England we will calculate on that basis. Most newspapers carry the values of foreign currencies at least once a week.

Accommodations: You have a lot of control over this, and Chapter 2 describes in detail how to get the best lodgings at the most reasonable prices. *Stay away* from big-name hotels or American chains if you want to save money, and instead choose a small tourist hotel for stays of less than a week. Rent a flat for trips of a week or more. Finding a comfortable, convenient place to stay in London for less than £20 ($32) per person/per day is easy. A better, and very realistic, figure to shoot for is £15 ($24). And good shopping can cut that figure by even more. If you can rent a flat and pay just £12 per person/per night for a family of four, you've found the equivalent of about a $70 per night motel room, except it will have three times the space, plus cooking facilities, which will save you even more money.

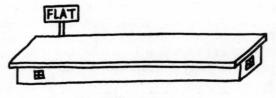

Some flats are just that

Planning Is the Key

Food: Chapter 5 is filled with tips about how to eat well inexpensively. If you stay in a small hotel, chances are a vast breakfast will be included in the cost of the room. A light lunch, mid-afternoon snack, and tasty supper can be had for £10–12 ($16–18) per person, perhaps less. If you rent a flat, you should easily be able to prepare two meals a day at home and eat one out for under £10 per person. Of course it's nice to splurge once in a while, and you can build that into your budget if you're inclined to do so.

Attractions and Sightseeing: It's harder to generalize about this because every family will have different interests. Note that some of the best attractions in London are free. The fabulous British Museum, with its mummies, rare books, and Rosetta Stone, costs nothing. Neither does the National Gallery, one of the world's great art museums. Picturesque walks along the River Thames or through the quiet Inns of Court are free for the taking. There's no fee to watch the Changing of the Guard, and a Sunday at Hyde Park watching the rabble-rousers at Speaker's Corner and examining the artists along Bayswater Road is free to one and all.

Many lovely churches and historic buildings are either free or have very low admissions. Westminster Abbey, where people have been worshipping for 800 years, is free, although entrance to the Royal Chapels—burial places of kings and queens, saints and scientists, poets and politicians—costs a little. St. Paul's Cathedral costs £2 to tour, plus a small additional fee to climb up into the dome, something not for the timid or easily winded!

Of course some attractions are more pricey. The Tower may cost £8 ($13) per person, but student and family admissions are available to reduce the cost. Buckingham Palace, which opens several rooms to the public during August and September, costs nearly $16 per person. But there are many wonderful attractions available for much, much less. Chapters 10 to 17 of this book will show you the best of them.

We wouldn't budget more than £6 ($10) per person/per day for admissions. Some days you'll spend more than that, but some days you'll spend nothing at all. Add in special extras. For example, if you want to see a play in London's West End (the equivalent of Broadway, only with twice as many choices) great tickets are available at half price on the day of performance. A daily average of £10 per person should cover everything easily, and it's no trick to make do with half that.

Shopping: Here's one place where we can't give you any clear idea of what you'll spend, because we don't know your tastes. Your total here might range anywhere from nothing at all to hundreds of dollars. If you're doing this on a tight budget, keep this category to a minimum. Give each of the kids £20 for special souvenirs and tell them that they must use their own money for anything beyond that. Don't start buying as soon as you hit British soil. Take your time and look around. Usually the most memorable things you buy aren't the most expensive but the little guidebooks to a place you particularly loved, or an inexpensive memento that evokes a mood. Some of our favorites include a £2 hand-dipped candle from a royal palace, a copy of the Lord's Prayer printed in an old Celtic language that cost 16 cents at an ancient church, and a well-worn but authentic 500-year-old Henry VII penny bought at a street market for £8.

Local Transportation: Buy a week's pass for the subway system, called the Underground (or more commonly, the Tube). Cost will be about £12 for a seven-day pass in the central area. Paying by the ride costs much more in the long run, more than £1 per trip. Passes are also good on buses in Central London. Chapter 6 will show you how easy local travel is, and how walkable London is. We also recommend that you take one quick trip out of town for every week of your vacation, and a railway ticket will take you to one of a dozen fascinating places that will be among the most memorable parts of your trip. Chapter 17 gives you complete information on those.

So here's the Lain bottom line for an economical per person/per day London experience:

Projected Daily Expense Budget per Person

	Reasonable Minimum	Outlandish Maximum
Accommodation	£12	£20
Food	£ 8	£15
Attractions	£ 5	£10
Shopping	£ 5	£15
Transportation	£ 3	£ 3
Total	£33	£63

What we're saying here is that once you're in London, your family can manage nicely on £33 per person/per day. That's about $53 apiece for lodging, all food, entertainment, and souvenirs. For a family of four, that's about $1,500 for a very comfortable week. For $2,500 a week your family could very nearly stop thinking about money altogether. I don't believe anyone in our family has *ever* averaged anywhere close to £63 per day, but I know that during longer stays we've certainly spent many days at *less* than £30. And remember, that pays for *everything*, including your hotel or flat. As we progress through the chapters of this book we'll be providing dozens of tips on having more fun for less money.

Planning Your Trip

In the last three chapters of the book you'll find everything summarized to make your planning as easy as possible. You'll find a list of our top family attractions, suggested itineraries that take into account the varied interests of family members and the uncertainties of the weather, and an expanded budget worksheet so you can project your expenses when you put together your plans for your vacation of a lifetime.

There's one more critically important element to planning a trip like this that we haven't talked much about yet, but it's central to your family's enjoyment of the vacation: total family involvement.

Everyone needs to participate. Taking a family abroad can be a complicated task if family members aren't excited by it and don't know what's going on. That's one reason we suggested in the Introduction that you wait until all your children are at least ten years old. The more everyone helps with the planning, the more excited by the trip and the more committed to having a good time they will be. When you look at the lists of attractions later in the book and decide on your itinerary, make sure that everyone gets his or her first choice represented on the list.

On any vacation, but still more on a foreign trip, everyone needs to be committed to the idea of just relaxing and enjoying the experience. Not everything will always go right on *any* vacation. But people who have had a hand in the planning are better able to shake off the unexpected, shift gears, and go on. Is a special attraction you wanted to see closed for renovation? That's a disappointment, but from planning you know of two of three other worthwhile things in this part of town. Take a walk over there and see one.

Informed travellers are flexible travellers. Flexible travellers may have ideas in mind about what they want to see and do, but they're not tied to a clock and a schedule, but seize the experiences they have with excitement. Informed and flexible travellers have more fun at whatever they do. So let's start planning . . . .

Recommendations

✔ Consider a trip at spring break or as early in June as possible.

✔ Plan your budget in advance on a per person/per day basis for easiest comparisons.

✔ Make sure the kids have money of their own. They'll spend it more carefully than if all they have to do is ask for money from Mom or Dad.

✔ Involve everyone in the planning to heighten anticipation and commitment to having a good time.

2. *Where to Stay*

I n this chapter we're going to tell you how to stay economically in London. It's easy to spend a huge amount of money very quickly on your lodgings, but it's just not necessary. We'll show you how to find a comfortable, clean, safe, and convenient place to stay that will not only save you money but will add to the pleasure of the trip.

Remember what we said in Chapter 1: First, there are seven million people who live in London. Very few are millionaires. If *they* can afford to live in London, you can too.

Also, remember that London is one of the major tourist destinations in the world. While many of the city's visitors are well-off in their own countries, London hosts far more tourists who are no better off than middle class. If *they* can afford to stay in London, so can you.

There are many types of accommodations to consider, probably more options than you'll find in most places at home. We'll discuss the advantages and disadvantages of the best possibilities here, giving you a good picture of what you can expect and how much you'll pay. Usually we'll break the cost down to an amount *per person/per night*, a good way to spot the best values.

What Are the Options?

We'll discuss four types of accommodations here:

- luxury and first-class hotels
- tourist hotels
- bed and breakfast homes (B&B's)
- flats (apartments)

The hotels we talk about in this chapter are used as examples typical of the class. They are included as examples only, not as endorsements. We can't afford to stay at a lot of these places either!

Luxury and First-Class Hotels

It's easy to find a hotel in London. Some of the finest in the world are located there. The Ritz has given its name to a word that's synonymous with elegance and luxury. Claridges has been the home away from home for visiting royalty from a dozen countries. The Savoy is world renowned. And of course there are the Hilton and Four Seasons hotels we expect in any world class city. And they can easily cost £250 to £300 a night or more for a double room. That's $400 up, or for a family of four that's more than $100 per person/per night, a cost that's out of sight for most families!

It might cost even more than that. Putting an extra person in a room frequently costs £20 or more each per night. But even at just £250 per night, that's still £1,750 ($2,800) per week.

Hotels are expensive because they sell you a lot of things you probably don't need to buy. Somebody will come in to make your bed every day. You get to use a different towel each time you take a shower. Your building has a grand lobby with expensive furnishings and a well-equipped exercise room, full secretarial service, and maybe a masseuse on duty 12 hours a day. A large proportion of their guests are business travellers, staying there on somebody else's money, or high rollers used to being pampered. That's probably not what you want to pay for on vacation with your family.

Where to Stay

If you can afford to live that way at home, go ahead and stay at the Dorchester. But most of us can't. Besides, staying in a fancy hotel in London isn't much different from staying in one in Chicago or Montreal. You're insulated from the very thing you came to experience, the life of another culture. There are better alternatives.

Less expensive hotels with fewer amenities are available, but even a more modest hotel can cost £85 to £100 a night or more for a room. This is the choice most American tourists make. A room that costs £90 per night sounds like a bargain by London hotel standards, but that's still a cool $1,000 per week or, for a family of four, $36 per person/per night. American tourists can be seduced by the familiar names of Holiday Inn or Marriot. Those are good hotels, reliable and as comfortable as their American namesakes, but they're still expensive for a traveller on a budget. We *still* can do better in two ways—space and cost—ways that are both cheaper and more fun.

Tourist Hotels

There are hundreds of small, tourist class hotels in London. These places don't have grand lobbies, massage tables, or 24-hour room service. What they do have is clean rooms in safe, often residential surroundings, simple furnishings, and *much* lower prices. Americans don't stay there as often, but Europeans and travelling British do, and they save a lot of money.

It's impossible to list all such hotels; guidebooks that try to do so go very quickly out of date. But the section "Finding a Hotel or Flat" in this chapter shows you several ways to go about it.

You won't get a mint on your pillow

How much can you save?

There are many hotels where a large room suitable for four people might cost about £70 per night. Your room will have a color TV, toilet, shower, and phone, and an English breakfast is included every morning! The breakfast can be wonderful, as you can see from the sidebar on this page. That £70 per night equals about $28 per person/per night. The total comes to about $780 a week, a savings of two thousand dollars over a luxury hotel! What have you given up? A famous name, crystal chandeliers in the lobby, and a mint on your pillow. You will have a comfortable room, possibly one that is more convenient than it would be at Claridges, and it will probably be larger.

But a room in a hotel, even a large, inexpensive room, is still a room. If your family is old enough, for only a little more money you might rent *two* rooms: one for the parents and one for the kids. Two double rooms at such hotels, each with its own TV and bathroom, might cost £80 to £100 per day total, or less than $900 per week. While that pushes the price back up to about

---

The World's Best Breakfast

This may be the time to say a word about the full English breakfast we mentioned above. Nobody does breakfast like the English. Outside of fancy and expensive hotels, lodgings usually include breakfast, and what a treat it is—enough food to keep you going all day.

You'll usually start with juice and a choice of coffee, tea, or milk, and be offered a selection of cold cereals while the rest of your breakfast is being cooked. When it's ready, you'll get eggs (choice of fried or scrambled), several pieces of toast with butter and marmalade, thick slabs of bacon, fat English sausages, and probably several things that will surprise you: grilled tomato, mushrooms, and (honestly!) baked beans.

We've often waddled out of the breakfast room well able to skip lunch entirely, making do with just a bit of fruit or cheese until dinner. Even if Denny's served this sort of breakfast, it would probably cost ten dollars. In England it comes with the room—in less expensive places! We still haven't figured out how they do that!

$32–$35 per person, per day, it's still substantially less than fancy hotel prices, and while you don't get that mint on your pillow, you've got twice as much room and the price *still* includes that fabulous breakfast.

Even greater savings are possible at many hotels if you're willing to share a bathroom. While hotel rooms without bathrooms are rare in the United States, they're quite common in the rest of the world. If you're travelling with children, a bathroom might be a convenience you want to pay for. But if you're trying to travel as cheaply as possible, it's a good option because it will normally reduce the cost of a room by £3 to £5 per night or more.

It may be possible to get adjoining rooms, one with a bathroom and one without, saving a bit more money

A Word About Bathrooms

Asking for a bathroom might not get you what you want!

In most of Britain, the word "bathroom" means a room with a bathtub in it, period. It might have a toilet in it, too, but it might not. Americans are generally squeamish about using the word "toilet," but the British aren't, so asking for the "bathroom" may get you a puzzled stare in a restaurant, which is unlikely to have a bathtub for its customers' convenience. Asking for a "rest room" will perplex anyone.

Be direct. Ask for the toilet, although asking for the "W.C.," the "Ladies," or the "Gents" will also get you where you want to be. Public toilets in tourist areas are sometimes announced as "public conveniences."

In seeking accommodations, note that not all rooms in inexpensive hotels and B&B's come equipped with American-style bathrooms. If a room is advertised as having a shower, it will not necessarily have a toilet as well. A room with all the plumbing fixtures is usually listed as "en suite" or as having private facilities.

for a family. The usual ratio of sleeping rooms to bathrooms in inexpensive hotels is one bathroom for about every three sleeping rooms. You actually sacrifice little in the way of privacy. We once shared toilet and shower rooms with two other guest rooms for five weeks and found the facilities occupied only twice during our entire stay. That's probably less often than it happened at home when our family was young!

A week's stay at such a hotel could be less than $700 for a family or four, just $25 per person/per night, and a full English breakfast is included!

Bed and Breakfast Homes (B&B's)

Staying at a pleasant B&B is one of the nicest parts of travelling around Britain. You stay in private homes as a guest of someone who rents out anywhere from one to a half-dozen rooms each night to travellers.

B&B's have a relaxed, homey feel to them and offer a pleasant way of meeting ordinary British people. B&B's are usually in residential areas and usually have some of the most immaculate, cheery rooms you're likely to see. Many have en suite facilities, but those with shared bathrooms cost a little less. And the breakfasts (have we mentioned breakfasts?) are fabulous.

While veteran travellers make extensive use of B&B's, staying in one in London probably isn't the best idea for a family that's spending a week or more in the city. We've used B&B's for one- or two-night stays in places where we've been seeing the sights, but they charge by the person and you can usually find cheaper long-term accommodations elsewhere.

In Central London, B&B prices of £25 or more per person/per night are common, although it's certainly possible to do much better than that. The Earl's Court and Notting Hill areas west of Hyde Park are havens for backpackers and have many less expensive B&B homes. If you take an overnight trip out of the city it's usually not difficult to find convenient B&B's for £12 to £20 per person/per night. But there's one more accommodation option to consider, and the one we think is ideal for a family vacation: Rent an apartment.

Flats and Apartments

Hotels are nice, but they're not very much like home. B&B's are nice and they *are* home—but somebody else's home. If you're spending a week or more in a city with a family of four or more, there are terrific advantages to creating a *home away from home* by renting an apartment (the English call it a "flat") for your stay. It gives you privacy, room to spread out, and can save you a considerable amount of money.

While housing can be expensive in London, the city's compact size and the ease with which you can get around make the major attractions accessible from all parts of town, and provide many possibilities for finding a short-term apartment. It's a fairly simple task to find a flat for £750 ($1,200) or more per week, but with only a little digging you can probably reduce that by as much as half.

For a family of four, a two-bedroom flat will suffice and a one-bedroom flat *may* be all you need, because the sofa may well open up into a sleeper that will accommodate two people. Bedrooms will most often have two single beds, or less often, a double bed. A family of four can be quite comfortable in such a flat.

Try to accommodate everyone

If your family is larger, one bedroom may still be enough. A couple of years ago we rented a one-bedroom flat for five. It had a sleeper sofa and the manager added a folding rollaway bed. We brought our own bed linens for it and he made no extra charge. The price was £400 per week, only £11.41 per person/per night— just $18.25. The flat was in a lovely residential street of Georgian townhouses less than a fifteen-minute walk from Parliament.

Better than the basic price is the fact that a three-room flat gives a family room to spread out. You're sharing a bathroom with the same people you always do, and your flat will come with a complete kitchen. This is another big money saver!

It's fun to eat out, but doing so day after day can leave us yearning for a familiar home-cooked meal. It's also expensive. As we explain later, finding economical restaurants in London isn't difficult, but lunch for a family of four will still cost close to £20 ($32) and dinner will probably be £30 (almost $50). You might not want to spend $80 a day for meals and if you have your own flat, you don't have to.

An ideal strategy is to fix breakfast in the flat—cereal, toast, eggs, whatever your family normally eats. Breakfast is a quick and inexpensive meal to prepare. After breakfast, set out for the day's sightseeing, taking along a snack for when the munchies strike.

Lunch is an inexpensive meal to buy. Pub lunches are quick, cheap, and tasty, sandwich shops are plentiful, and fast food places abound. Finding lunch for less than £5 per person is easy.

After a day of soaking up London, you can go back to your flat and relax, fix a simple meal of something familiar, talk about the day, watch a little TV, and, if you're up to it, charge off again, rested and well-fed, for an evening activity. Your flat will come with all the cookware and dishes you need and there *will* be a market just down the street to buy food. Chapter 5 goes into much more detail about this.

Of course you'll probably go out and have an evening meal at a restaurant a few times, but you can save lots of money by cooking often in the flat. Instead of that £30 for a meal for four, you can buy the ingredients for a simple and tasty supper for £5 or £6, saving yourself $30 to $40 a day.

Kennington Park is a large neighborhood park south of the Thames

What do we recommend? We think that, especially for a family staying a week or more, renting a flat makes wonderful sense in terms of cost, spaciousness, privacy, and comfort. You just can't beat having your own living room, separate bedroom, and a kitchen with refrigerator and stove. A suite like that in a hotel would probably cost as much per night as the flat will cost per week. Flats are available at any time of the year, and while renting one is not quite as simple as calling a hotel reservation desk, the comfort and savings make the small amount of extra effort worthwhile.

Just as good as the cost savings is the fact that you'll be *living like a local*. Much of the fun of travelling is to experience the culture of the place you're visiting, and frankly, staying in a fancy hotel in Moscow isn't very much different from staying in one in New York. Especially in a place like London, where you can speak the language and read the signs, it makes good sense to become as much a part of the city as you can. It makes for a much more intensive,

satisfying experience, and one that leaves you with a deeper understanding of your host country.

A flat can be ideal even if you're not bringing the kids along on
this trip. Smaller studio or efficiency apartments, often called "*bed-
sits*," are available for as little as £200 per week. That's less than $23
per person/per night for two people, and provides more of that
home-away-from-home feeling than a hotel.

We provide some budget worksheets in Chapter 20 that permit
you to compare the costs of your trip with a variety of lodging and
meal options. It's clear, though, that renting a flat is an economical
option that brings exciting London within the reach of millions of
people who never dreamed they could afford it.

Finding a Hotel or Flat

London is an easy city to get around in but we recommend that you
seek a place in Central London. You might save a little money by
going to the outskirts, and for a stay of a month or more the savings
might make the extra travel time worthwhile. But every
neighborhood in the city has its own charm and history, and London is a very walkable city. Staying in the central area allows you to
take advantage of that.

The area we suggest is roughly Zone 1 on the Underground, the
area north of the river
that's enclosed by the
Circle Line. You can
go from one end of this
area to the other in
about 30 minutes on
the tube, and wher-
ever inside that zone
you stay, you'll find
many interesting or
historic places an easy
walk from your flat.
The sidebar, "London

London Neighborhoods

*It is often said that London is a city of villages,
and the more time you stay there, the more you
recognize the truth of the adage. The boroughs
and neighborhoods of Greater London have highly
individual characters, and when you look for lodgings, it helps to know a little about the area.*

*We should say this about safety: We've walked
in many corners of London at all hours of the day*

Neighborhoods" in this chapter offers a quick tour of the areas we're talking about.

We will *not* be recommending specific hotels or apartments. Guidebooks that do, become useless soon after publication. (Although we hope you'll buy the *next* edition of this book too, we don't want to be obsolete before you've made *this* trip!) Hotels come and go, and available flats change from week to week.

What we *will* do is tell you how to find a place to stay, how to do the research for getting just the right place for your family. We'll give you an address and telephone number to get you started, and some advice on what to ask for.

Finding a Luxury Hotel

Here's one section where we *won't* be

and night and never felt threatened or uneasy. Nevertheless, follow sensible safety precautions wherever you are—busy city streets at noon or quiet residential streets at midnight.

Now let's visit the neighborhoods in Zone 1 of the Underground, north of the river. We'll move roughly east to west through the area.

The City: There's a difference between the city of London and the City of London. Normally in this book, when we refer to the city of London we mean the entire metropolitan area, what the locals call Greater London. But capitalize the C and you have something much more specific.

The City refers to the oldest part of town, the part that was once enclosed by medieval walls. It runs from just west of St. Paul's Cathedral to the Tower of London, and from the River Thames north to the Barbican. It's often called "the Square Mile" because that's roughly its size.

You're not likely to find accommodations in the City. It's the financial hub of Europe, and bustles madly during the day, but few people actually live there and its streets and shops are deserted at night. Even the majority of pubs close by seven o'clock, and finding a late bite to eat is nearly impossible. It's a lot like Wall Street in New York City.

The City is surrounded by areas called **Whitechapel, Spitalfields, Barbican, Clerkenwell,** *and* **Holborn.** *You might find accommodations in the latter three, but they are busy areas that are often less touristed and with fewer options for visitors.*

Islington: *A bit north of the City is the almost suburban area of Islington. There's nothing glitzy* giving much advice. Because we don't recommend spending the money on such posh digs, places definitely *not* designed for families on a budget, we'll leave it at this: If you want to stay at this sort of hotel, most of the other London guidebooks have the addresses and phone numbers you need; those books are available at your public library. Enjoy your mint!

Finding a Tourist Hotel

There are almost a thousand hotels listed in the London Yellow Pages, and there are others that aren't even included there. How can you choose a good hotel from the hundreds that are available? While most budget hotels are clean and well-run, it would be a shame to travel so far and wind up in

or pretentious about the area, which tourists seldom visit. There are few hotels but you might be able to find a flat here for less money than you would pay in the trendier parts of town. Regent's Canal meanders through Islington and provides a peaceful footpath for a quiet walk or morning run. It's inhabited mostly by ordinary, pleasant, hard-working Londoners.

Bloomsbury: This is a prime area for both students and tourists. The colleges and halls of the University of London are here, and Bloomsbury has at its center the magnificent British Museum, one of the great museums of the world. Probably no comparably-sized area of the world has housed so many noted figures of literature and the arts. There are dozens of hotels in all price ranges here and lots of short-let flats, which may be a bit more expensive than in some other areas of the city.

Soho and Covent Garden: Here is the entertainment center of London. This is where you'll find hundreds of restaurants, clubs, music halls, theatres, cinemas, and some less savory entertainment. The streets are busy 24 hours a day. The area is frequently crowded and noisy, but it's fun and safe. The police have been largely successful in running the prostitutes and drug dealers out of the area altogether, and the few remaining sex clubs and peep shows promise far more than they give. It's less rowdy and far less sleazy than New York's Times Square area.

There are a number of budget hotels in the area and many flats. Prices vary quite a bit. Some flats a pigsty run by somebody who figures that because you're just passing through they won't get your repeat business anyway.

A little research is all that's necessary. Start early so you can send off for information, then look carefully at what you receive.

Start with the London Tourist Board. If you write or telephone them, they will send you their book *Where to Stay in London*, an excellent resource. The book lists about 400 hotels in London, arranged geographically. The book is a goldmine of information, providing basics like address, phone, and fax numbers, of course, but also a description of the property, the number and sizes of rooms (important for finding a family place), the number with private bathrooms, meal availability, credit

near Covent Garden can be expensive but good bargains are available, too.

Marylebone: Pronounced Mar-lu-bun, *this is an area with as many accommodation possibilities as Bloomsbury but without the intellectual pretensions. In some places Marylebone is a hodgepodge of different ethnic groups, with Arabs, Indians, Pakistanis, Jews, and West Indians living peacefully together, but other parts are high-toned and exclusive, a refuge for doctors and other professionals. Accommodations of all types are available in Marylebone. The proximity of Paddington Station means that travellers are common and presented with plenty of options.*

Mayfair: If you want to live in elegant surroundings and run the risk of living in the same building with the rich or titled, this is the place. Mayfair hotels are the most opulent and flats are the most luxurious. We won't claim that it's impossible to find economical accommodations here, but it's more difficult. Don't write the area off as a possibility, but be careful you don't end up just paying for an address.

Westminster, Belgravia, Pimlico: Westminster, of course, is the seat of government, and these areas are home to many government employees and numerous foreign embassies. There are some very expensive areas here, but there are also good bargains to be had. Some of the best tourist class hotels can be found in Belgravia, and there are many short-let flats, some priced very reasonably and others at more inflated prices. At the center of the district stands Victoria Station, one of the cards, a summary of hotel facilities, and current prices. Their address and phone number is:

London Tourist
Board
26 Grosvenor
Gardens
London, SW1
U.K.
phone 011–44–171–
824–8844

The guide also includes ratings from the London Tourist Board, but the ratings are not especially useful. Hotels are rated from "Listed" to a maximum of five crowns, but those ratings refer only to the *type* of facilities the hotel has, not to its quality.

Slightly more helpful are quality grades, which range from *Approved* to *Deluxe*. But the absence of these ratings does *not* mean the hotel is a poor one. A large number of hotels do not participate

chief railway terminals and the point at which the vast majority of arrivals to Gatwick Airport enter London, since the direct train from Gatwick arrives here. In fact, the old neighborhood names of Belgravia and Pimlico are gradually being replaced by a more general Victoria.

Chelsea: *Another nice area near the river, Chelsea has many flats, but the prices are somewhat higher in this upscale area. Chelsea has almost as many literary and artistic associations as Bloomsbury; notables like Thomas Carlyle, James McNeil Whistler, and Oscar Wilde once lived here.*

Kensington, Knightsbridge: *Like Mayfair and Chelsea, this is a tony area, but because there are so many places to stay, it is usually possible to find lodgings that aren't too much more expensive than other areas. This is prime shopping area, with Harrod's and many of London's most expensive and exclusive stores nearby. But the area has wonderful museums too, and is close to Hyde Park. Kensington Palace, home of assorted members of the Royal Family, is here, and dozens of foreign embassies dot the area.*

Notting Hill, Earl's Court: *At the west end of our tour, you may find good prospects here for budget accommodation. It's known as a transient area, and there are many tourist hotels and flats available. The area is a mecca for the young seeking a bargain place to stay and the shopper seeking bargain prices: the bustling Portobello Road Market is here. You'll have no trouble finding a variety of inexpensive restaurants here, either.*

in the rating system and are as good or better than those that do. (Example: The Dorchester, one of London's poshest hotels, where single rooms begin at £220 per night, is not rated.)

In the most recent edition of the LTB book, there are 46 hotels located in Central London which have family-sized rooms and prices of less (sometimes much less) than $25 per person/per night.

Once you've looked through your LTB book and narrowed your choices, telephone the manager! It's not as expensive as you think (some rates are now as low as long-distance calls within the U.S.) and $20 worth of phone calls will give you a better feel for what a hotel is like than any guidebook.

Not only are you able to learn more

Every neighborhood has its advantages. Some are near shopping, some are close to museums, some are in old and historic areas. But inside Zone 1 you're seldom more than a ten-minute walk from a tube station and a 30-minute ride to anywhere else in the zone. Inexpensive restaurants and pubs for meals will be close by, as will public parks and squares for picnics and for the kids to release their bottled-up energy. London is a city made for living, no less for the tourists than for Londoners themselves.

Telephoning England

For quicker service, consider telephoning England. A five-minute phone call can now cost less than a dollar and your questions can be answered at once. Your best bet is to get up early and call before 7 a.m., when the daytime rates go into effect. Remember the time difference: England is five hours later than New York, eight hours later than California, so 7 a.m. in New York City is noon in London, while 7 a.m. in Los Angeles is 3 p.m. in London.

To call London directly, first dial 011 (the international dialing code), then 44 (the country code for England), then the area code (for London it's either 171 or 181), and the local number. The call goes through as quickly as a long distance call in the United States and the connection is usually just as clear.

When the phone is ringing on the other end, you'll hear two short rings at a time, instead of the one long ring you hear in the U.S.

about what the hotel is like and check availability of dates, but you can discuss the rate. (The manager may call it the tariff.) The published rate is not necessarily the lowest available, and a friendly chat with the manager, coupled with a request for a lower rate will often produce good results. It's worth a try!

If the hotel takes credit cards you may be asked to guarantee your stay with a card, but in some places you'll save money if you pay for your stay in cash on arrival. Some hotels charge a fee of as much as 10 percent to accept credit cards and a few places won't take them at all. Seven of the 46 hotels mentioned above do not take American credit cards.

If you can't use a credit card, you may have to go to your bank and have them prepare an international money order. An ordinary personal check, drawn on an American bank in dollars is of no more use to them than a British bank check in pounds is to you.

Note, too, that a confirmed hotel reservation may be considered a legal contract in many places abroad, and if you cancel, the hotel is legally allowed to collect the full price of the booking unless they can rent the room. This is seldom a problem, but you might consider trip cancellation insurance. It's not expensive and the agent who handles your household insurance, or any travel agent, can help you.

Finding a B&B

As we've said before, a B&B stay might not be the most practical or economical approach for family travel. If you'd like to investigate the possibility, however, or if you're travelling without an entire family, the LTB book lists several agencies under the heading "Accommodations with Families." A letter or telephone call will get you all the information you require.

If you take an overnight trip to another city in Britain, you might like to try a B&B. We've never booked one ahead, although for a large family during the tourist season that would probably be a good idea. We stop at the tourist information office at the railway station when we arrive and let them find a place for us, a service that usually costs just a pound or two. By using their experienced people and their extensive listings of B&B's in every price range and part of the city, we've never been disappointed. They can also book a B&B for you for the next night in the city you plan to visit tomorrow.

Finding a Flat

We consider this the best option for a family of four or more, but it also takes the most planning. It's not difficult, though, and the rewards are worth it.

There are scores of estate agents (real estate agents) in London who also handle apartment rentals, and there are about 50 hotel and apartment booking companies. Some work only for a limited number of landlords and some represent hundreds of properties. It's also possible to request information from the many apartments and holiday short-let companies which advertise in magazines like *In Britain*, a method of finding accommodation that many people, including the authors, have had great success with.

But an easier approach is to return to your LTB book. The most recent edition lists 31 agents with about 1,200 apartments available for short-term let. The book briefly describes what's available and gives a price. Don't take the price too seriously!

First of all, some listed prices were cost *per day* while others were cost *per week*, often with no indication of which were which. And when we checked, every manager we spoke with offered a price that was different from the published price, and many were *lower* than what the book said.

Use your phone as a tool

Use your telephone as a tool. Find four or five flats that seem to offer the best combination of facilities, location, and price and telephone the managers. If you call during off-peak hours, you can get plenty of information from five different apartment managers for less than $15 in phone charges and have an excellent feel for what you're getting. Here are some questions to ask:

1. I'm looking for a 1- or 2-bedroom flat sleeping 4 for the week of July 10. The flat should be inside the Circle Line. What can you offer me?
Be specific about the dates or, if you can be flexible, say so. Give the size of the flat you want and keep in mind that you may be able to save some money by taking a flat with fewer bedrooms as long as the flat has a sleeper sofa that can accommodate some of your family.

2. Does the price include VAT?
The Value Added Tax, a sort of sales tax, is present throughout Europe. The rate in Britain is currently 17.5%, so if the price you're quoted does *not* include the tax, you'll need to figure it in to get a fair comparison with flats that do include the tax.

3. Describe the furnishings and contents of the flat.
You'll want to know if bed linens are included (they usually are), what sorts of kitchen supplies are available (usually simple place settings, a few pots and pans, and basic cooking utensils), and other sorts of furnishings like sleeper sofa, telephone, television, and alarm clock are available. Ask whether the bathroom includes both a bathtub and a shower if that matters to you. You can ask if the flat is air-conditioned, but air conditioning is uncommon and seldom needed. Even July and August temperatures seldom go above 80 in London and nights are usually breezy and cool.

4. What's the address of the flat? What's the nearest tube station?
It's nice to be able to spot it on your map to see where you'll be relative to London attractions and to see how simple transportation is to other parts of town. Londoners tend to identify neighborhoods according to the nearest tube station.

5. *Where are the nearest grocery store, self-service laundry (laundromat), and produce market?*
Most flats won't have a washer and dryer, though some places will have a few washing machines available to residents. There are small markets in every neighborhood, but your landlord can tell you just where.

Armed with the information you gather from landlords, you ought to be able to make a good decision about where to stay. Telephone the landlord again and confirm the dates and the price, and see if you can get it reduced further. A five-person family might well get a four-person rate if they bring along a sleeping bag and the kids take turns camping out on the floor. Offering to pay in cash rather than by credit card will frequently get a discount. Just being cheerful and flexible and clearly enthused about the prospect of spending time with your family in this exciting city may influence the landlord to knock off a few pounds.

One more thing. By renting a flat you've saved hundreds of pounds over fancy hotel costs. Remind yourself of that, and when you go to the grocery store on your first afternoon in London, spend two pounds and treat your family to a box of mints.

Recommendations

✔ For stays of more than a week, look for an inexpensive flat. They *do* exist!

✔ For shorter stays, consider a tourist class hotel. It is always possible to find accommodation for less than £20 per person/per night.

✔ In a flat, fix your morning and evening meals at home most of the time. In a hotel, load up on the free breakfast.

✔ Use the telephone to make arrangements. It's the quickest and most efficient means, and will save you money.

3. The Art of Travelling

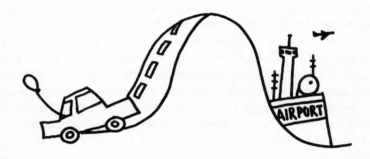

Travelling sounds so easy. Go to the airport, sit down on a plane, take a nap, walk off. Simple. Maybe that works pretty well for the carefree single, but hauling a family halfway around the globe takes a bit more planning. Still, the task needn't be intimidating, and ought to be fun. We've said before that *planning* the vacation is the second best part, exceeded only by the trip itself. In the next two chapters, then, we'll talk about finding an airfare that will leave you with extra money to spend once you arrive in Britain, about how to pack for the trip, about how to navigate immigration and customs when you arrive, how to get to your lodgings, and what your first actions should be when you arrive.

Finding the Best Airfares

This is the single most expensive item in your trip, probably accounting for more than half your total expenses. It pays—literally!—to do careful shopping. Usually that will involve the help of an experienced travel agent.

We see a growing mindset among some people that goes something like, *"Hey, I can use the computer and get just as good a deal as a travel agent, or better, because I won't be worried about a commission."*

That could be true, but seldom is. It's true that most travel agents are paid according to a percentage of their sales. But a good agent has much more incentive to save you an extra $100 and get your repeat business and word-of-mouth recommendation than to get an extra five or ten dollars commission. An experienced professional knows more of the subtleties of travel than you have time to learn.

What you want is an agent with *international* experience. Ask "How many international trips have you sold this year? Tell me about them." Or, "How many times have you travelled to Europe? Where have you gone?" An agent who specializes in cruises probably *won't* leave you very much better off than if you do the work yourself, but one who specializes in international travel can save you hundreds of dollars.

Here are some tips for planning your trip that can help you and your travel agent get the best fare for your family. Note that there is one common theme that runs through all of these: *Flexibility*.

1. *Avoid high season, if possible.* Fares are highest during the summer. If, as we said in Chapter 1, you can go at other times of the year, you can often cut your fare by more than half. Low season is during the winter months. "Shoulder" season corresponds roughly to late fall and early spring; fares are higher than during low season but better than those during high season.

2. *Don't travel on weekends.* Flights on Friday, Saturday, or Sunday may cost $20 to $50 more apiece each way, or up to $400 for a family of four that flies both directions on weekends. Schedule all your flights Monday through Thursday.

3. *Stay between seven and thirty days.* Supersaver fares, normally your best bet, usually require a stay in that range. Shorter stays can still be reasonable *if* you stay over on a Saturday night.

4. *Be willing to drive a little to save money.* The fare from your hometown airport and from one 75 miles away can be different by hundreds of dollars. Have your agent check the fares from other nearby cities as well as from your hometown.

5. *Flights with connections may be cheaper than non-stops.* Most people prefer non-stop flights, so airlines may offer a lower rate if you're willing to change planes en route.

6. *Ask about consolidators.* These are companies that buy seats in advance, at a discount, from regularly-scheduled airlines, and then sell them to consumers at a lower profit than the airlines do. There are good companies and bad ones, but a travel agent with international experience will have worked with many, will know their reputations, and will be able to shop for the best price among them as well as among regular airline listings. But you may need extra lead time and flexibility to take maximum advantage of these.

7. *Watch the rates on foreign carriers for good savings.* If you live near a city served by many international carriers, this is a possibility—again, if you're flexible. Icelandic Air, for instance, like some foreign carriers, sometimes has spectacular rates to London . . . *if* you're willing to make a 24-hour stopover in Rejkavik. If that appeals to you, great! Usually the only way to save money on a deal like this, though, is if you can drive to a city served by that airline. If you have to fly from Michigan to New York to catch your plane, however, the cost of your domestic flight will probably eat up your savings.

8. *Watch frequent flier deals.* Our travel agent once led us to the new and as yet unadvertised frequent flier program on British Airways which allowed us to consolidate all our family's mileage in a single account, rather than under an individual account for each person. (As far as we can tell, they are *still* the only company that does that.) The program also had generous sign-up mileage bonuses and extra miles for the first trip. The result was that one family trip to London on British Airways produced enough frequent flier miles for completely free round-trip low season tickets for Mom and Dad later. It's hard to beat a deal like that.

The ultimate frequent flyer

9. Watch for sales. Airlines are like other businesses—they compete, sometimes ruthlessly, with other companies. The demand for international flights in the summer has been so high in the last five years that there have been few real sales, but there often are during low and shoulder seasons. Have your agent check regularly for them because they are frequently not advertised, are limited to just a few seats per flight, and disappear as unexpectedly as they appear. If you've bought a ticket at more than the sale price, airlines will often exchange it for the sale price, perhaps adding a service charge of $25 to $50 a ticket. But that may still result in a substantial savings for you.

Getting the lowest airfare takes some time, work, and vigilance by

---

A Packing Checklist

Unless you're going for a shorter time, seven or eight days worth of clothes is the maximum you ought to need. Some things can be washed out in a sink and will dry overnight, and many items can be worn more than once. If you're staying for more than a week or so, you'll have little trouble finding a coin-operated laundry within a short walk. There's no need to pack the entire contents of your closet. Here's a quick guide to what you might take along, and where to carry it. Remember that you've got more clothes than are listed here: You're wearing clothes on the flight over!

Checked Suitcase
o *Men: 1–2 pairs trousers; Women: 1–2 pairs of slacks and/or skirts*
o *5–6 shirts or blouses*
o *underwear for 7–8 days*
o *8–10 pairs of socks/hose. After a long day on your feet, fresh socks feel good.*
o *sleepwear*
o *1 pair of shoes*
o *sweater*
o *outerwear appropriate to the season*
o *Men: optional jacket and tie; Women: dressier outfit*
o *handkerchieves*
o *towel if not provided with lodging*
o *toiletries*

Carry-on Bag
o *change of clothes in case baggage is delayed*
o *guidebook*

o *camera and film*
o *any electrical equipment: radio, travel alarm, etc.*
o *hearty snack*
o *book or other in-flight entertainment*
o *medical supplies, prescriptions, sunglasses*
o *your trip diary*

On Your Person
Never pack the following in your checked luggage. They should be carried in the safest place possible—with you.
o *passport*
o *moneybelt or pouch with cash and travellers cheques.*

Other Items to Consider . . . and to Leave at Home
Here is a list of other things you might consider. Some of these are things you should certainly take, and others are things we suggest you leave home as more trouble than they're worth.

An umbrella—*YES*
England is often rainy, especially in the winter, and a folding umbrella will probably get occasional use at any time of the year. (carry-on)
A folding tote bag—*YES*
A fold-up bag or string bag that can be shoved in pocket or purse can be handy in shops that are less free about giving bags to customers than American shops are. They're also good for toting around a lot of little souvenir purchases. (checked bag)
A washcloth—*YES*
The British seldom use them (they call them

you and your travel agent, but can pay hundreds of dollars in dividends when you board the plane. Like shopping for the best accommodations, it's a matter of deciding what you want and how flexible you can be, and then doing enough research and asking good questions. We've never minded this part of the planning process, though, because the more research we do, the more the process helps to build the excitement and anticipation of the trip.

Pack Light. No! Even Lighter!

"Well, I might need this if it rains, and this if it's cold, and I should take an extra paperback in case the plane is delayed and . . .."

If this sounds like you, you've got a lot of company. You can always spot the tourists who've overpacked. They're the ones whose heavy suitcases make it possible for them to tie their shoes without bending over. Packing light is really simple. Lay out on the bed everything you think you'll need, then reduce the pile by half.

That's *not* a joke or an exaggeration. Cut it in half. Take comfortable clothes that travel well, stick to one basic color and its complements so anything can be worn with anything else, and pack clothes that you can wear in layers to be prepared for either warm weather or cold. These are standard pieces of advice, and they've become standard because centuries of tourists have found them true. We have a friend who has travelled extensively who suggests, "Pack everything you plan to take two days ahead of time. Then carry all your luggage

face flannels) and they probably won't be supplied with linens in hotel or flat. (checked bag)

Blow driers and curling irons—*NO*

The British use 220 volt power rather than the 110v we're used to, and the plugs are shaped differently. You can buy an adaptor but even a good one may give unsatisfactory results, making something take too long to warm up or burning it out. They're probably more trouble than they're worth, but if you must have one, consider buying an inexpensive one in London. It'll probably cost less than a first class power converter.

Medicines—*YES*

This is especially true if you take any sort of prescription drugs. Bring them in the original container from the pharmacy, and bring a copy of the prescription itself, preferably referring to the drug by its generic name. Brand names may be different in other countries. Otherwise just bring a minimal amount of aspirin or other over-the-counter remedies. If you need it, you can buy it abroad. (carry-on)

Radio—*MAYBE*

If you have a small transistor radio, your kids might enjoy listening to British stations in the evening. You'll hear more classical music, less country, less talk, and more drama than you will at home. Be sure the radio has analog tuning, though. Most inexpensive digital radios sold in the U.S. are adjusted to American frequencies, but stations are spaced differently on the dial in England. (carry-on)

Addresses—*YES*

A nifty trick is to write out the names and

addresses of people you want to sent postcards to ahead of time—on sticky labels! Then you won't forget anyone and can just slap the labels on cards as you write them. (checked bag)

Guidebooks and maps—YES

But not everything. Books are heavy. Take one or two books you know you'll refer to (this one, for example!) and the maps we'll show you how to get from the British Tourist Authority. (carry-on)

Games—YES

Take along a pack of cards, a Gameboy, maybe a couple of books of puzzles to use on the plane or for a family card game when you're relaxing in the evening. Each child ought to take something he or she will enjoy doing. Flights from the U.S. to England run six to ten hours. That's an awfully long time to sit patiently.

Extra suitcase—MAYBE

If you have a suitcase that can be folded small and tucked into your luggage, take it along. If you end up buying more souvenirs than you expected you can fill the extra bag with dirty clothes and put the mementoes in your sturdier luggage. We have a couple of carry on bags that expand into suitcases we can check, just in case. (checked bag)

Inflatable pillow—YES

These come in handy as an extra pillow in case the one in your hotel or flat is too . . . well . . . flat! They're also soothing to slip behind your back halfway through your cramped flights over and back. (carry-on)

around the block. If you can do it, you've packed well. If it's too heavy, you've over-packed." We endorse that advice.

What Clothes to Take

It's OK to wear a shirt more than one day without washing it if the weather's cool. Underwear and hose can be washed out in the sink and dried overnight. One dressy outfit is plenty, maybe more than plenty: If you *are* invited to tea with the Queen you can do what most people do—*rent* formal clothes. Only the very pricey restaurants require jackets and ties; most places prefer what the British call "smart casual." All that usually means is that jeans not be shredded and that shirts have collars. People seldom even dress up for the theatre any more, especially in the summer.

Resist the temptation to overpack

For general sightseeing, neat, casual clothes are fine. You won't see shorts as often as you do at home, especially on men, and the people who wear them in the city are almost certainly tourists. But you aren't likely to need them anyway. The summer temperatures in London seldom go above 80, and top out in the low 70s most days.

One thing you shouldn't try to minimize is shoes. Don't try to get by on just a single pair, no matter how comfortable it is. You'll walk much more than usual and spend more time on your feet. You'll be more comfortable if you bring two pairs of shoes and switch off every other day.

No one will think it odd if your kids wear the standard international uniform of youth—jeans, tee shirts, and sneakers (usually called *trainers* or *plimsolls* in Britain). But make sure they have "smart casual" clothes for when they want to look a little sharper. Take a look at our *Packing Checklist* in this chapter.

How to Pack

The airlines will allow you to check two bags per person plus bring one carry-on onto the plane. That's what you're *allowed* to take, but that's crazy! Unless you're going for a month you don't need that much. Come to think of it, we *have* gone for a month and not taken that much! Keep the number of pieces of luggage to a minimum. Mom's and Dad's clothes should go in one suitcase. Things for the kids can go in another suitcase, or maybe two smaller ones. Unless your family numbers more than six, don't take more than three suitcases. If you do, you're carrying more than you need.

You can also take carry-on luggage, and every family member ought to do that. A carry-on bag might be as small as a gym bag or a full-size carry-on. Check with your airline on the permitted size, but if the length, width, and height of the bag totals 45 inches or less, you ought to be safe.

Every person should have a change of clothes in his or her carry-on, just in case your luggage takes a vacation of its own and travels to a different airport. Include a book to read, a book of games or deck of cards, or other items to keep the owner occupied. Each person should carry an emergency snack. The Minneapolis to London flight of one member of our family was once kept on the ground for three hours while an engine was repaired. Passengers weren't allowed to leave the plane and dinner was delayed for four hours. It was after 10 p.m. when the plane took off, and 11 p.m. before 350 hungry, cranky passengers got their dinner. A bag of trail mix or something else filling should be in every bag.

Also put any electronic equipment you're carrying in your carry-on, because it makes it easy to inspect. Airlines aren't keen on seeing baggage with batteries and wires inside checked luggage. So carry your radio, Walkman, travel alarm, and similar items in the carry-on. Also carry your camera and film with you where it's safer, less prone to being tossed about, and easily inspected. Don't put your money, tickets, or passport in checked baggage *ever!* The best place for those things is on your person or in the moneybelt we'll tell you about in Chapter 7. Once you're aloft, your ticket and passport can go in your carry-on.

Always put your name and address (and address in your destination city) inside your luggage as well as on your baggage tag. Even carry-on luggage should be identified in these ways.

They Have Stores in England

If you forget something, there's no need to panic. They've had stores in Britain for quite a number of years now and anything you can buy at home you can buy in London. It will add to the adventure to use new brands of toothpaste or deodorant.

Memory Makers: Pictures and Diaries

Of course you'll take your camera. The pictures you take will be treasured mementoes of the trip. We always take plenty of film with us because it's cheaper over here, but if you run out you won't have any trouble buying more in England. But this is important: Invest $15 in a lead-lined film bag. Inspectors are supposed to hand-inspect film bags on request but they sometimes refuse and demand that the entire carry-on go through the x-ray machine, promising that their equipment won't hurt your film. But it will, especially if you're carrying very high speed film. (We usually carry several rolls of ISO 1000 or 1600 for use in museums or cathedrals.) When they spot the lead film bag on the x-ray they'll hand inspect it anyway, and you may have saved your film from fogging or discoloration. When you come back to the States after your trip, remember to put all your film, both exposed and unexposed, back in the lead bag.

It's a good idea to carry the bill of sale for your camera with you, if it isn't American made, especially if you have a very expensive camera that looks fairly new. If you can't prove that you bought it in the United States, the U.S. Customs inspector can make you pay duty on it when you return to this country, just as if you had bought it abroad. If you no longer have the bill of sale, the Customs office in any international airport in the U.S. can give you a certificate of ownership before you leave on your trip.

Let the kids take a camera, too, that they can share or use on a rotating basis. They'll take pictures of different things than you will. Seeing Dr. Who's TARDIS might not mean very much to you, but it might be a highlight of the trip for one of your kids.

Give every member of your family one other memory maker: a notebook. Keeping a trip journal is just as important as taking pictures of the trip. Even if you've never kept a diary, try it on this trip. Set aside fifteen minutes every evening for journal writing. Record where you went and what you did, but also make a note of interesting things that happened. You can have people answer questions like these:

Today's Date:
What and where I ate:
 Breakfast—
 Lunch—
 Dinner—
What was today's weather like?
Here are the places I went today:
Here's the neatest thing I saw or did today:
Here's the worst thing that happened today:
Here's the funniest or strangest thing that happened today:
Here's what I bought today:
Here's what I thought about today:

Encourage, but don't force, everyone to keep this kind of a journal. If they do, we promise that it will be as precious to the owner as any photographs in years to come. But let the kids keep them confidential; they don't have to share their thoughts if they'd rather not.

Making the Most of Travel

The act of going from place to place was probably more fun when it was more leisurely. With the arrival of the airplane, however, transportation became something more to be endured than enjoyed. The best things about transatlantic flights is that they compress several days of crossing the ocean into several hours squeezed inside a metal tube. It may not be fun, but at least it's fast. But there are some things you can do to help everyone get more out of the experience, even to set a positive tone for your vacation.

The Art of Travelling

Enjoying Your Layover

Most people will react to a headline like that, "Enjoying Your Layover," in the same way they would react to a pamphlet from their doctor titled "Enjoying Your Appendectomy." But it is possible to enjoy the experience. (The layover, that is; we have no opinion on appendectomies.)

Unless you live near a city that has non-stop air service to London, you'll have to fly to a city that does. There's probably nothing more boring than spending hours in an airport between flights, but with luck you might be able to get a headstart on your vacation with creative use of a layover.

Because of jam-packed flights a few years ago we were forced into an eight-hour layover in Philadelphia on our way to London. Fortunately there's a fast, efficient subway from the Philadelphia airport straight to downtown. When we got in, we stowed our carry-on bags in a locker, then headed downtown to see Independence Hall, the Liberty Bell, and other sights we'd never seen in person. We spent five hours trooping around the historical sites, had a leisurely late lunch, and got back to the airport in plenty of time to check in for our 9 p.m. flight. Seeing some of America's key historical sites set a wonderful tone for our trip, and gave us the opportunity to get some exercise before our seven-hour transatlantic jump.

Many airports have similar rapid-transit connections between the airport and downtown. If your gateway city does, it might be worth taking an early flight just to create a sightseeing layover.

What if there's no way of going into the city for your layover? Try to make the gap between flights as short as possible, of course, but also bring along a game or two that will engage the whole family. Card games like Uno and Miles Bornes, little magnetic chess and checkerboards, and trivia games are easy to carry and are fun for the family. Younger children will often be amused for quite a while with people-watching games like seeing who can find the most different college sweatshirts on people passing by, or who can come up with the most complete list of major league baseball team hats on the heads of their fellow passengers.

You might also consider bringing a roll of quarters. There's sure to be a line of video games in the airport that will keep some of your crew occupied for a good portion of your layover.

Here's one more valuable tip about layovers, compliments of several veteran travellers: If possible, do *not* travel through Kennedy Airport in New York. The international terminal at JFK is the country's busiest and while you probably won't have many problems *leaving* the country, returning to the U.S. is often a trial. Lines at Customs and Immigration are long, and you ought to schedule at least a three-hour layover between the arrival of your international flight and the departure of your connecting flight home.

Enjoying Your Flight

An old joke asks "What's the difference between a plane full of transatlantic passengers and a can of sardines?" The answer, of course, is that the sardines have room to stretch out. Airlines squeeze as many people as they can aboard each plane because more passengers means more profit on the run. So unless you can afford to fly business or first class, expect to be a little uncomfortable. The payoff at the end will make the cramped quarters bearable.

That's fine logic easily understood by adults and older children, but younger family members have a harder time being patient. It's difficult enough to get them to sit still for a half-hour at home, much less for eight hours where even a wiggle is tough to do. Still, a pleasant trip is not too much to expect if you plan ahead and let the kids know what to expect.

Most flights to Britain from the United States leave in the late afternoon to mid-evening hours, landing in London between 6 and 10 a.m. That means the flight is overnight, giving everybody a chance to sleep. That's fine in theory but it seldom works out so neatly. Consider a fairly typical seven-hour flight from the East Coast.

The plane takes off at 7 p.m. About 7:30 the flight attendants bring around the beverage cart, offering complimentary soft drinks, cocktails, and wine for dinner. Your meal probably won't be served until at least 8:30, so if you're used to eating earlier, get a snack while you're waiting to board your plane back at the airport. Half an hour or so after the last meal has been served, maybe 9:15, the crew turns down the cabin lights for the movie. You may see a couple of shorts like a news summary and a travel video, followed by the movie feature. These video presentations will last at least two hours, making the time on our flight about 11:15.

That seems like plenty of time for a good sleep before morning landing, right? But don't forget that London time is five hours ahead of the U.S. East Coast. When it says 11:15 on your watch, it's really 4:15 a.m. in London already. Since this is a seven-hour flight and you've already used more than four hours eating and watching the movie, you're left with less than three hours of sack time. And don't forget that the flight attendants will be serving breakfast 60 to 90 minutes before arrival. If there's as much as two hours where nothing's going on, you're on a very unusual flight.

Just the bustle of life five miles high will usually be enough to make children forget their cramped space for a while, especially if they have done little flying before. Get them a window seat if possible, not so much because there's much to see on an overnight flight, but because they're not hemmed in with people on both sides and so feel less cramped. Having the wall to lean against when they're ready to go to sleep will make them more comfortable and so more likely to sleep.

Check a few days ahead with your airline to see if they can provide a meal with more familiar foods for children. Almost any kid would rather have a cheeseburger and fries than the cornish hen with some fancy French sauce on the regular menu, and most airlines are happy to accommodate such requests.

Try to persuade children to skip the movie and try to sleep, but if they can't go to sleep right away, they can dip into their carry-on bags for some entertainment. Get them to leave the headsets off when the movie starts and they'll probably lose interest in the film quickly. Instead, they can listen to favorite tapes on a Walkman, play with a Gameboy (but without sound, please, for the sake of fellow passengers), read, draw, or play quiet games with the family member sitting beside them.

Encourage children to take out their trip diaries and make the first entry, talking about how things have gone so far, what the plane is like, how the meal was, what they did in the airport waiting to board the plane, what they're most looking forward to, and so on.

Asking a child to sit still for hours on end is difficult, but if the child has been in on the planning of the trip and is told what to expect on a long flight, he or she is much more likely to be a pleasant and congenial travelling companion. With luck, from the window seat your child will be the first to spot the green coast of Ireland in the morning as you fly by on the way to London. That moment when land is spotted is when all the stiffness of hours of forced immobility begins to melt away. We've crossed an ocean!

For the latest updates to *London for Families*,
check our page on the World Wide Web at

http://www.as.udayton.edu/com/faculty/lain/lonfam.htm

---

4. Arrival!

There's no feeling quite like that of waking to glorious bright sunshine on the first day of an exciting vacation after an all-night flight over the ocean. The brilliant blue sky and dazzling sun above and, if you're lucky, the lush green of Ireland below, set exactly the perfect mood for an exciting holiday.

The flight attendants may be around with hot towels for freshening up, then will serve you a simple breakfast. They may turn on the movie screens again, this time for a video about stretching tired muscles in the cramped confines of your seat, and follow that up with a short film about what to expect when you arrive at the airport.

Attendants will also pass out an arrival card for you to complete. It merely asks for your name and home address, your nationality, the purpose of your visit, the flight you're arriving on, and where you'll be staying in Britain. The cards are simple, but if you have any questions the cabin crew can help you. This is standard procedure on entering almost every country; you'll even have to complete a similar card when you re-enter the United States.

At the Airport

Chances are you will arrive either at Heathrow Airport, which is about 15 miles west of London, or at Gatwick, about 25 miles to the south. Either way, the process is the same and involves a good deal of standing in line (or "in a queue," as the British would put it).

You'll go from the plane to immigration. When you get to the front of the line your family will be told to go together to the inspector's station where you'll hand over your passports and arrival cards. The inspector will ask you a few questions, like the purpose of your visit and how long you intend to stay. Don't be nervous; this is a routine procedure. But don't joke around and waste the inspector's time; he or she has to talk to several hundred arrivals today, and just wants to be assured that you really are nice, normal people who have come to spend a holiday and some money in Britain.

Your next stop will be the baggage claim area where you'll pick up your luggage. Nothing to do here but to stand and wait for your bags to come out. Probably all your suitcases except one will come off the plane within five minutes—and the last one will be the final bag off the plane 20 minutes later. We've often wondered how they do that.

Once you've grabbed your luggage, follow the crowd: They're all headed to Customs. (On the way, you'll make a happy discovery—baggage carts are free!) You'll find three lines in the Customs Hall. Unless you're

> ***Tip:*** *Unless you've travelled on the same plane with 350 other people before, you may not have realized how many similar-looking suitcases there are in the world. Before you leave home get two colors of bright plastic mending tape. Put a colorful tape pattern on both sides of each family suitcase and you'll spot your bags immediately with no guesswork, and no one else will pick up your luggage by mistake.*

bringing in some taxable goods like more than a bottle of alcohol or a carton of cigarettes, follow the Green line, which means you have nothing to declare and pay import duties on. The Red line is for people who are bringing such things into the country, or are bringing in items they intend to sell. The Blue line is for citizens of other European Union countries.

It's possible, but unlikely, that a customs inspector will stop you to inquire about what you're bringing into the country. As long as all you're carrying is legal items for your own use, you'll have no difficulties. To tell the truth, we've *never* met an unfriendly Customs inspector in any country.

That's it. Once you clear Customs, you pass into the Arrivals Hall and can really begin to feel like you've arrived in England. The formalities of immigration and customs might take as little as 20 minutes or as long as an hour, depending on crowds, but once you've passed through, your vacation can really begin.

Getting to Your Lodgings

You have many better options for getting into town

First step is to get into London, and how you do this depends on which airport you flew into. But you'll get your first taste of Britain's efficient public transportation systems. At each airport your options vary somewhat, so we'll talk about each. It is worth noting that you'll usually be expected to pay your fares in British currency, not with American money, credit cards, or travellers cheques.

Getting into London from Heathrow

At one time nearly all U.S. airlines flew only to Heathrow. That's no longer the case but you have several possibilities for getting into the city from here.

1. The Airbus: Big red double-decker buses leave every few minutes from in front of the terminal. Just follow the *Airbus* signs. The buses run on two routes. The A-1 bus runs south of Hyde Park through the Kensington and Knightsbridge areas of London, ending at Victoria Station. The A-2 bus runs north of Hyde Park along Bayswater Road and Oxford Street, up Woburn Place, ending at Euston Station or Russell Square.

In either case, look at your London map before you leave and determine where you can most conveniently get off the bus to get to your hotel or flat. If you've packed well, a walk of a few blocks shouldn't tax you too much, and might feel good after hours of being cooped up in plane and bus. If it's too far to walk, you'll have no trouble hailing a taxi to take you the rest of the way for just a few pounds.

Cost of the Airbus is about £6 per person one-way. The trip can be slow, especially if you arrive early enough to have to plod through rush hour traffic, but perched in the upper deck of the bus, you'll get your first glimpses of London.

2. Taxi: This isn't a very economical alternative for three people or less, but if your group includes as many as five people, you might save a little over the cost of five fares on the Airbus plus taxi.

London black taxis are an experience in themselves. They're big and boxy, but very roomy and comfortable. The drivers are first-rate and have a comprehensive knowledge of the city. We'll tell you more about the taxi system in Chapter 6, but they're a good option for a larger family at this point. Fare into the city will be in the £25 to £35 range. There will be a taxi rank directly in front of the terminal. Join the queue and wait your turn; it will take just a minute. Stick to the black cabs. There are unlicensed "minicabs" that may solicit your business but their fares are unregulated and their drivers less well trained. The regular London taxi driver is unfailingly honest and efficient.

3. *The Underground:* If you long for a little more adventure, if you're travelling light, or if you've been in London before and are comfortable with the idea, you can take the Underground or "Tube." (Note: The English don't call it a *subway*, which to them means an underground walkway for pedestrians.) The Piccadilly Line of the tube system extends to Heathrow and provides the most economical way into the city, about £4. Just follow the signs that say "Underground" or have the familiar London Transport logo (-O-).

Maps of the tube are available at every station and in many London guidebooks. The system is easy to use. There are twelve color-coded lines that cover every corner of the city. Find the tube station nearest to your destination and note what line it's on. See where that line intersects with a change station on the Piccadilly Line. That's the route to take. When you get off at your destination station you might be close enough to your lodgings to walk; if not, hail a black taxi in the street and you're probably only a short ride and a couple of pounds away from your flat or hotel.

Taking the tube probably isn't for the group on its first trip to London, travelling with a half-dozen suitcases. It's the fastest and cheapest way into the city as a rule, however, and is a London institution in itself. Everyone from shop clerks to members of Parliament rides the tube, and you'll quickly discover its many advantages.

Note that since you'll probably be arriving in the morning, it's fortunate that Heathrow is the beginning of the Underground line. You should be able to get seats together for your group, and you'll be able to keep your luggage close at hand. The train will get crowded very soon because it's rush hour.

London for Families

Getting into London from Gatwick

Ten years ago Gatwick Airport was used mostly by charter flights and flights from other cities in Europe. That's no longer true. Regular flights from major U.S. and British carriers now arrive at Gatwick each day, where passengers find an airport that's a bit less sprawling and crowded than Heathrow. It's a little farther from the city than Heathrow is, too far to make a taxi an economical option, but it has a first-rate transportation link: the Gatwick Express.

The Gatwick Express: When you enter the Arrivals Hall at Gatwick, turn and look to your right. At the far end of the room you'll see a large, bright yellow sign for the Gatwick Express. That's your destination. The Gatwick Express is a train that runs non-stop between Gatwick Airport and London's Victoria Station 24 hours a day. Except in the middle of the night the trains leave the airport every 15 minutes and take exactly 30 minutes to get to Victoria. The service is convenient and efficient, and gives you a chance to get your first real glimpse of the English countryside.

(To tell the truth, the scenery on the trip isn't very inspiring. There's little green English countryside, no quaint villages, not a single castle. There are a few rather ordinary towns and some rather industrial areas, but don't worry: the good sights will come soon enough.)

Tickets for the train are available from trackside machines and from a counter at the entrance. If you're staying in England for less than a month, get a "London and return" (not "round-trip") ticket, which will cost you a bit less than two one-way fares. The return ticket is good for 30 days. Just keep it with your airline tickets. Price of a one-way ticket on the Gatwick Express is about £9. Note: *You cannot buy tickets on the train in Britain the way you sometimes can in the United States. All passengers must have tickets when boarding. On this train, however, you are usually able to pay on board. If you're in doubt, ask an attendant on the platform.*

It is possible to take a coach (bus) from Gatwick into London for two or three pounds less, but the trip is much slower. Coaches arrive at the Victoria Coach Station, adjacent to the railway station. We prefer to take the faster and more comfortable rail link.

Thirty minutes after you set out from Gatwick, you will arrive at Victoria Railway Station. You've got a couple of options for getting to your hotel or flat from here, and they're similar to what we discussed earlier.

The most convenient approach, and probably the cheapest option for a family, is to take a taxi. There's a separate taxi rank for the Gatwick Express, so it's not even necessary to go into busy Victoria Station, which will be very crowded at this time of the morning. A taxi will take you almost anywhere you need to go in central London for less than £10 from Victoria, and that includes the small supplemental charges for extra people and luggage. It's this taxi ride that will probably give you your first look at some familiar London landmarks. Depending on where your lodgings are you might find yourself driven past Buckingham Palace (quite near to Victoria) or Trafalgar Square, or catching a look at Big Ben.

By the way, there's little reason to fear that you'll be "taken for a ride," except to your destination, by your taxi driver. London cabbies are probably the best in the world and licenses are so difficult to obtain that operators are not going to risk their livelihood by charging you £50 for a £5 ride. The black taxis are highly regulated and are safe and reliable.

Experienced London visitors might want to venture onto the tube from Victoria Station (the Victoria, Circle, and District lines are available here) but the tube will be very crowded at the time you're most likely to arrive, and you may have trouble keeping all your family and luggage together. If there are more than three people in your group, you probably won't save money, either, unless your hotel or flat is pretty far out of Central London. Not much doubt about this decision: Taxis are the way to go.

Moving In

Well, you're here! You've landed in England, made your way past the inspectors in the airport, probably used at least two public transportation systems from a list that includes the bus, taxi, train, and tube, and you've found your hotel or flat. You've talked to the person in charge and moved into your temporary lodgings. You made it! Now what?

We're going to give you some difficult advice. You've just spent a large amount of money on many hours of more or less uncomfortable travel over several thousand miles. What you want to do now is get to the payoff: *Let's go see something!* We probably can't talk you out of that, but here's how we recommend that you spend your first six hours in London.

Hour 1—Get moved into your lodgings. Unpack and put things away. It will be more difficult later when you're really tired. You need to move a little more slowly than you normally would to give your body a chance to recover from the rigors of the trip and to reset itself to its new time. If the time in London right now is 11 a.m., remember that in New York it's only 6 a.m. and in California it's still 3 in the morning. Your body is struggling to resolve the conflict between the time it feels like and the time you're trying to adjust to. Take it slowly; by tomorrow you'll be caught up.

A little jet lag is normal

Hours 2–3—This is the hard part. Unless you got four hours of sleep on the plane, have a snack now, then take a nap. You're tired. Even if you're too excited to be aware of it, your body's stretched pretty thin right now. If you can get the kids to lay down for fifteen minutes, they'll fall asleep. So will you. Most people don't sleep very

Arrival!

well or very long on the plane unless they do a *lot* of travelling, and you can reduce your physical and emotional stress with a nap right now.

Set an alarm, though. Under no circumstances should you sleep more than two or three hours. It's important for your adjustment that you get a good night's sleep at normal hours tonight so accept the fact that you'll be just a little foggy today. Unless you're performing surgery, that's OK. When the alarm goes off, get up and get active, no matter how much you want to go back to sleep. If you oversleep now you won't sleep tonight and you'll have a Foggy Day in London Town again tomorrow.

Hour 4—You'll probably be up and around by 1 or 2 p.m., earlier if your flight was one of the very early arrivals. Now is the time to begin a little gentle sightseeing. We still recommend that you not overtax your feet or your nerves by trying to do too much today. One or two people can be more aggressive tourists, but if you've got your family with you, you have to consider the stamina of the person who tires most easily. Children who are overly tired can take much of the enjoyment out of the trip for everyone else.

For example, it's a mistake to do too much walking today. We recommend later in the book that you do as much walking in London as possible because that's absolutely the best way to see the city, but that begins tomorrow. If you spend *too* much time on your feet today, you risk blisters, even from comfortable, well broken-in shoes.

You've spent many hours in the air today and the pressurization of the cabin, combined with your immobility, has caused your feet to swell, whether you've noticed it or not. Too much walking too soon will raise blisters

> ***Tip:*** *Find your neighborhood on a London map and photocopy an enlarged copy of it for every member of your family. On your walk on your first day in London, mark in the locations of important places in the neighborhood.*

or other sore spots and make your next week or two unnecessarily painful. It's important to stretch your legs, but the rest of the trip will be more fun if you don't overdo it today.

So what sights do you see? The nearest ones. Take a walk around your neighborhood, two or three blocks in each direction from your lodgings. These are the streets you'll get to know best, use the most, and feel most at home on during your trip, and now's the time to get acquainted.

To get the most out of a trip like this, we suggest that you try to "live like a local." That doesn't mean you're not a tourist, of course, but to really sample the many flavors of the place you're visiting, you should try to experience as much of the daily life of the place as you can. Travel isn't just about taking pictures of monuments and famous buildings; it's about learning how other people live. So as you walk around the neighborhood this afternoon, there are many things you should keep an eye open for and mark on your map. The feature "Who Are the People in Your Neighbor-

---

Who Are the People in Your Neighborhood?

One of your first jobs after moving in for your stay is to check out your new neighborhood. Here are some things to look for:

Grocery stores. *If you're renting a flat, you'll want to buy food. There will probably be one good-sized grocery store and several smaller convenience stores nearby. Even if you're not in an apartment, these are the places you will be visiting for snacks and treats occasionally.*

Tube stations and bus stops. *These are your gateways to London. Mark their locations on your map and note what lines each tube station is on. Notice which buses stop at the nearest bus stops.*

Restaurants. *You'll find a nice selection of restaurants of countless ethnic varieties in every corner of London. Note those that look interesting and are reasonably priced. You'll find menus posted in the window. They'll give you somewhere close to go when everyone is weary and it's hard to make decisions.*

Pubs. *As we explain later, pubs in England are much more than drinking establishments, they're neighborhood social centers. They're also excel-*

hood?" tells you what to look for.

Hour 5—Eat a good meal. Pick one of the restaurants nearby and have a good lunch. You're famished by now, and you'll probably want to do this as part of your neighborhood walking tour, but if not, it's your next item of business. Relax, have something interesting to eat, have plenty of non-alcoholic beverages to drink to rehydrate yourselves, because flying dries you out more than you realize. After a nap, a short

lent choices for lunch, serving hearty, inexpensive fare. Kids 14 and up are welcome for meals in most pubs, but the drinking age is 18. Most pubs are open from about 11 a.m. until 11 p.m., though Sunday hours are usually more limited.

Self-service laundry. If you're staying more than a week, you'll need to wash clothes. A few flats or small hotels provide laundry facilities but probably you'll need to find a nearby launderette. Note the open hours. Laundries often close earlier than their American counterparts.

Newsagent. Looking at British newspapers and magazines is interesting and has some surprising twists. Britons read three or four times as many newspapers per person as Americans do, and papers come in all varieties from the solid and respected Times to the sensational Daily Mirror. A dozen or so daily newspapers are published in London, and looking at the papers is part of the travel experience you shouldn't miss.

walk, and a meal everyone will feel the best they've felt all day.

Hour 6—Shop. If you're staying in a flat, now's the time to buy groceries. Even if you're in a hotel, stop at a grocery store and replenish your supply of snacks. It's fun to wander through the aisles looking at the unfamiliar foods and brands. Stop at the newsagent and buy a couple of newspapers and the magazine *Time Out*. This excellent weekly magazine is an indispensable guide to everything that's happening in London each day, from rock concerts and operas to walking tours and lectures. It contains complete information on every movie and theatre program in the city and includes a description of the major tourist attractions, along with open hours and admission prices.

While you're shopping, also stop at the nearest tube station and buy a London Transport tube and bus pass. If you're staying for a week or more, the pass will require a passport-size photo. TravelCards, available for up to a week are also available but are not valid weekdays until after 9:30 a.m. The cost changes each year but tube and bus cards will cost about £12 per week, maybe the best deal in town. Chapter 6 describes how to buy and use them.

Finish your first six hours in London with a little relaxation at your flat. Don't go to sleep, but relax, read the paper, check out the TV or radio programs, and take it easy for a half-hour. Then, if you feel like venturing out, do it . . . but don't *over*do it. Pick one place, maybe Parliament or St. Paul's or Westminster Abbey (which is across from Parliament anyway) and go visit. But finish your sightseeing early today, have a relaxed supper, sit in a park this evening if the weather is good, and go to bed by 10 o'clock. Tomorrow you'll wake up refreshed with your body clock set on London time, ready to do some more serious sightseeing.

There is one potential problem. What if your hotel room isn't ready when you arrive? One friend just hops on and grabs a seat at the top of a double-decker bus and goes for a ride. She gets to sit and relax and to do some sightseeing at the same time. After a while the bus will bring her back to the place she started from. When we've stayed at a hotel, we check our bags, then take that stroll around the neighborhood, shop for some essentials, and check into our room as soon as it's ready.

Travelling successfully with a family is different from travelling alone. You need to give much more attention to preserving everyone's good humor and cheerfulness. It doesn't seem like anyone could be crabby or impatient when presented with the array of exciting sights that somewhere like London affords, but that array is actually part of the problem. There are too many choices, too many new experiences all at once, and that's stressful for adults—so imagine how much more stressful it is for kids. Ease into the city and everyone will enjoy the subsequent days all the more.

Recommendations

✔ Take it easy your first day in London. Don't wear yourselves out trying to do everything immediately, but get settled in and get to know your neighborhood.

✔ Take a short nap after arrival and get to bed early the first day to reset your body clock.

✔ Limit your walking today and you're less likely to be plagued by blisters later.

5. Food, English Style

If you've heard anything at all about British food, it's likely to have been negative. British food is stereotypically starchy, fatty, and greasy, with a special emphasis on their beloved beefsteaks, which are generally cooked to the point of blandness. (In fact, one derogatory term for an Englishman in France translates as "beefsteak"—of course, the French are notoriously more stuck-up about food than the English . . . and perhaps about everything else as well.)

You'll be glad to know that this stereotype is more often than not simply false. There is plenty of wonderful food and drink out there—and the very best of it, as we've continually emphasized, can be cheaper than you think. In fact, one thing that you probably *don't* want to do, if you want to get to know England, is go to a "fancy" restaurant. Chances are that the main courses will be French anyway . . . or some chef's idea of French.

There's just so much more out there, places the whole family can get into. And unless you live in New York, you'll find more variety here than you would at home. This chapter will tell you, we hope, how to feed yourself and your whole family well, British-style, inexpensively. (And you may discover that this subject is as close to our hearts . . . as to our stomachs.)

Food, English Style

Your Local Market

Once again, we urge you to scout out your neighborhood on the day of your arrival. Among the many things you will discover on your stroll will be a grocery store. (And there *will* be one nearby. You may wish to ask the person who gave you the keys to your flat or room. Don't be afraid to ask at any other shops you may find in the area.) The market will probably look like a small grocery or large convenience store. There are big American-style supermarkets—Safeway is a well-known chain in Britain, and there are big local chains like Tesco and Sainsbury's—but it's more fun to go to the smaller shops, or the smaller branches of the big chains. There's sure to be one nearby.

Browse around. Some items you see may look very familiar, like Snickers bars, for example, which until recently were known as Marathon bars in the U.K. Some items will look familiar, but with a strange British twist, like Kellogg's Sultana Bran cereal instead of Raisin Bran. And other items, like cream of pheasant soup and canned haggis, will be completely new, the sort of things you'll never see at your local A&P or Kroger.

We recommend that you buy any necessary staples from all three of these categories. Remember, it's fun to be adventurous. Besides, even if none of you actually *like* cream of pheasant soup, at least you can say you've tried it! (However, you *may* want to pass on the haggis . . . .)

You may also wish to purchase munchies, such as candy bars, and picnic items when you stop in for the first time. Also, don't forget toilet rolls (a.k.a. toilet paper) if you need them back at the flat, and washing-up liquid. Unlike in the U.S., where we always use separate soaps for different uses, the British sometimes use an all-purpose detergent for dishwashing, laundry, etc. Don't try it as a shampoo, however.

One last thing before you leave the market—check its hours of operation. You'll want to return, so find out when it's open. Stores might not be open as late as the ones you're accustomed to at home, and 24-hour markets are harder to find.

Look Around You

We suggested earlier that on your first trip around the neighborhood, you might also want to see what restaurants are nearby. Chances are that you'll come across at least one, and there are sure to be several within a short walk. Take a chance! It may be that the nearest restaurant is a relaxed family-owned grill that won't be too different from home. It might be a shop that serves that famous British staple, fish and chips. It might be a foreign-looking ethnic restaurant (London, as the capital of the erstwhile British Empire, is renowned worldwide for its enormous variety of ethnic food.) Any of the above are well-suited for families with children of any age, and here's a *very important tip*: Restaurants are required by law in Britain to post their menus on the outside. How very thoughtful, especially for tourist families on a budget!

Finding a neighborhood restaurant is a good idea for a couple of reasons: You may be tired after a long day of sightseeing and craving a more familiar place to sit and eat, or it can serve as the "default" place to eat if the kids can't make up their minds.

How to Eat While Sightseeing

A good way to save money on a trip like this is to have a big breakfast. In an earlier chapter we talked about the Full English Breakfast, and if you're staying at a small hotel that offers one, take advantage of it and fill up. Then you might be able to get through the afternoon with just a snack or two. But if you're travelling with kids, they'll be hungry again soon, no matter how much you feed them in the morning. And when they get hungry, they get cranky. You don't need cranky on vacation.

So, you're tromping around London, thoroughly immersed in British culture, when suddenly the kids remark in a subtle manner that they are starving to death. You glance at your watch, and oops—it's way past lunchtime. What now?

Well, it depends in a large part exactly where you are. Most areas in London will have restaurants somewhere nearby. This may be your best bet, especially if your children are tired and need to sit down. We've had lots of fun eating out at lunchtime and cooking an evening meal back at the flat. We get to sit down when our feet are starting to get sore, and we save a substantial amount of money by *not* paying dinner prices for the same food we can get at lunchtime.

There are a few places in London where eating may not be as simple as crossing the street to get to the local Wimpy's, a local hamburger chain. But you'll probably have several options nearby.

Street Vendors

Vendors sell just about everything

Most London street vendors carry the familiar beef burgers. However, you may wish to be more adventurous and try a sausage roll, pasty, or meat pie. Prices are usually low, but the lines may be long at lunchtime. Selection may be limited to just a few items, but it's quick and easy. But except in popular tourist areas like Covent Garden or near the Tower, vendors may be nowhere to be found if it's not lunch or tea-time.

On-Site Food

If you're at a major tourist site when the hunger pangs strike, there may well be an on-site vendor or a restaurant in the museum. (Just another reason to take those free maps.) Prices and selection may vary widely, of course, but you can usually find something good at a reasonable price. Be careful, however, if offered a choice between a full-service restaurant and a snack bar. You may find it easier on your wallet to choose the snack bar, especially in higher-class places like museums. Sit-down restaurants like those in the British Museum or National Gallery serve excellent food but at prices that can approach £10 per person! Add to that the fact that the kids are less likely to enjoy that more complicated cuisine, you might be better off in nipping out to the courtyard in front of the British Museum or to Trafalgar Square in front of the National Gallery (or the equivalent place wherever you are at the time) and buying a sausage roll from the bloke with the pushcart! A sandwich, packet of crisps (bag of potato chips), and a soft drink will cost less than £3.

Pubs

Many pubs offer meals, but if you have children under 14 with you, this isn't an option unless they have a special dining area. But if you can, do have lunch at a pub once or twice. It's quick, filling, inexpensive, and almost always tasty.

Emergency Food

It's a great idea—perhaps a necessity—to stash easy-to-carry items in a purse or camera bag, especially if you have young children. You can find suitable items (candy bars, sausage rolls, meat pasties, etc.) at your grocery. However, if you're in a museum, church, or similar place, you'll be expected to wait until you're outdoors, just as you would in this country.

Tip: You can often find premade sandwiches at grocery stores.

The Lord John Russell in Bloomsbury is a typical neighborhood London pub

What to Expect from British Restaurants

So you're tromping around, and everybody's hungry, and you're surrounded by restaurants. (The ideal situation.) You'd probably like to know something about what to expect from where you eat. (Don't forget—read the posted menu! A quick check can save time, embarrassment—and your money.)

There are good family restaurants—among them are Garfunkel's and Angus—where you can sit down, relax, be served, and choose from a wide variety of meals. Prices and selection are about what you'd expect from a Bob Evans or Ponderosa in the U.S.

There are also some quicker, cheaper chains with less variety on the menu—such as Wimpy's—that are nonetheless relaxing and family-oriented. And London has its share of mom-and-pop restaurants as well that may have a limited menu but are usually very reasonable price-wise.

Ethnic restaurants, believe it or not, are usually an extremely safe bet. Many of these, too, are family-run establishments where your server will speak English to you but another language to the cook. Actually, here you may get the most and best food for your money, and unless you live in a large city, it will most likely be something you've never sampled before. However, if any member of your party has any food allergies or is a vegetarian, it's a good idea to mention that.

Tipping

A tip is usually known in the U.K. as a "service charge," and by law restaurants must print on their menus whether or not this is included automatically, as it often is, on the bill (known as a "check" in the States). If you have any doubts, ask your server. However, do not be fooled! If you pay by credit card, your slip will sometimes have a blank space for you to add the service charge, even if it has already been added to your bill. It would take really great service for us to tip twice, so pay attention.

Tips are usually about 10 to 12 percent of the bill, 15 percent if service has been exceptional. Even where a service charge is included, it is usual to leave loose coins from your change on the table. Occasionally restaurants will have a tip jar near the cash register instead.

(Of course, you should mention this at *any* eating establishment if there are any doubts.) Likewise, if you can't stand spicy food, it's best to inquire rather than take a chance at ordering something you may not want to eat (or ordering something, eating it all, and paying the price later).

Another great British tradition is the fish-and-chip shop. They serve just that, and sometimes chicken and occasionally a vegetable (other than potatoes—remember, a chip is a french fry. Potato chips here are crisps over there. Check out the glossary). The price is generally quite low—of course, so is the variety, but you might want to try it just once for the sheer Britishness of it all. Unfortunately, due to health regulations, these shops no longer wrap their wares in old newspapers, but don't worry—the newspaper-thick coating of grease over it all is still the norm, which is why your kids should love it.

And then there are the ever-present McDonald's, Burger King, Taco Bell, and so on. There's no shame in eating here if you're hungry. There, as here, the locations are specially scouted for convenience. And everyone might like a break for a more American meal. But we would urge you not to make a habit of eating in places like these, even if your kids prefer it. Remember, you can eat in a McDonald's at home. Why travel halfway around the world just to eat at the same places and do the same things? (And some people do just that. Sad, isn't it?)

One thing about McDonald's, Burger King, *et al.* in Europe —some people claim the burgers taste funny. There are several theories to explain this phenomenon (the kids may claim poison— *not* true), perhaps the

Eating Vegetarian

You might not want to eat everything

The main drawback of being a vegetarian in London is that it keeps you from tasting the local delicacies. Of course, some people would say that the main advantage of being a vegetarian in London is that it keeps you from tasting the local delicacies. Just contemplating the traditional British menu, with its fish and chips, bangers and mash, blood pudding, and haggis, can sound like a greasy, grisly affair to a vegetarian. (I have heard of vegetarian haggis, but since authentic haggis is a Scottish mixture of oats and sheep guts cooked in a sheep's stomach, I cannot imagine what the vegetarian version would consist of.) You might even think about boning up on the cuisine so you can laugh at your omnivorous companions as they eat this stuff.

But the real key to enjoying mealtimes in London is to eat ethnic. Remember, the British Empire stretched out through the Middle East, India, China, and beyond. Wonderful meals can be had at restaurants with exotic cuisines, and you won't even have to alienate your non-vegetarian compatriots. If these ethnic dishes are already familiar breed of cattle used in Europe (much more likely). We chalk it up to the fact that your palate has by this time been spoiled by the wonderful English fare, and will begin to demand better from now on. You decide, though.

Tip: The English, a perverse people, drink their beverages at room temperature. So if you want ice, ask for it. And if you want water to drink (it's not normally served at a restaurant.) ask for tap water. You'll probably get an incredulous look from the waiter, who'll bring it to you with a sort of grudging

to you, you'll find London's curries, stir-frys, and falafel among the best in the world. Otherwise, these are new experiences not to be missed. Even the worldliest traveller ought to be able to find something new to try in London.

Best of all, restaurants in London have menus placed prominently outdoors so you can make sure there will be something for you to eat before you walk in and sit down. Even if you're dragged into experiencing London's "pub grub," don't panic. There's always the ploughman's lunch—hearty bread and cheese—or perhaps a cheese and onion pasty. And don't forget to try the pickled onions.

Lastly, all warnings aside, don't be too skeptical. Allow yourself to be surprised. One of the best meals I've had in England was a delicious mushroom ragout served on a baguette in a small, unpretentious cafe in Stratford-on-Avon. Don't be afraid to ask what something is—they have vegetarians in England, too. And don't worry. You won't starve. In fact, you'll probably eat better than the rest of your travelling companions.

—Rik Lain

piece or two of ice. But it costs little or nothing. Mineral water (available everywhere in both sparkling and still varieties) will cost more than a pound.

A Few Words About Pubs

Undoubtedly you have already heard about that most British of establishments, the pub. Since there are already stacks and stacks of guidebooks about the pub experience, we'll only say a little bit here. First of all, a pub is not like a bar. There is a bar inside the pub, but it is not the be-all and end-all of the pub. You could describe the pub more accurately by comparing it to a VFW or Eagles post, only without the dues and ceremonies. In many towns and neighborhoods it is the primary center of local culture.

You can get a good, cheap, filling meal at many pubs, especially at lunchtime. There's usually not a lot of variety—usually a sampling of sandwiches and combinations of meat, vegetables, and cheese—and the quality varies considerably depending on where you go—but it is a most British meal. You'll usually find the day's menu on a chalkboard outside the entrance, on a chalkboard above the bar, or both. Expect to find a small variety of meat pies, perhaps an omelette, a couple of sandwiches, maybe bangers and mash (sausages and mashed potatoes), and a "ploughman's" (we here would spell it "plowman's") lunch. This last is a sampler of cheese, rich bread, cold vegetables, a pickled onion (delicious! try it!), and often some sort of meat, and you can easily tell that it's a laborer's lunch. It's simple, quick to prepare (and eat) but extremely filling and satisfying.

Because pubs serve alcohol, they usually

Alcoholic Beverages

While not all pubs serve meals, all serve drinks. What you can get depends on where you are, but there is a wide variety to choose from (18 and older only, please). British beers are confusing to us Americans because we use the term "beer" to refer only to lagers, the main commercially available type of beer in this country. The British commonly have several other types of beers to choose from, such as ales, bitters, and stouts, many brewed locally, even on the premises. If this interests you, you'll probably want to buy and pore over a guide to world beers before you go. For the rest of us, practically everyone's heard of Guinness (they sponsor the world record book) so you may wish to try it (although it is available in many places over here).

Another favorite is cider, which tastes just like the U.S. version, but with a kick. It's also extremely alcoholic, so beware. In fact, practically every British beer is more alcoholic than U.S. versions, so it's best to limit yourself to one or two pints. (Also keep in mind that the British pint is larger than the American pint.)

prohibit children under 14 from entering. However, sometimes pubs have a dining area separate from the bar area, and everyone's welcome here. Pubs that have this often serve a wider variety of meals. You can expect to pay more than for, say, a ploughman's, but the prices are mostly very reasonable and the food is home-cooked and delicious. A pub lunch will normally cost £3 to £5. A soft drink will cost about a pound and a pint of beer costs about £2.50.

Picknicking

From our trips to London, we think one of the best experiences your family can have in a sometimes bewildering, often hectic vacation (didn't we go to get away from it all?) is just to take time out, sit underneath a tree, open a bag full of picnic goodies, and do nothing for a few hours. It was a gorgeous Sunday, we hadn't planned anything special, we packed some fruit, some sausage rolls, and some candy, grabbed the *Sunday Times* and took the tube to Hyde Park. We probably spent 45 minutes horsing around, trying to find just the right tree. We sat in the cool shade, passed the food around, and did nothing but loll, reading the paper, talking about what we'd seen, just relaxing.

All families should have an experience this wonderful. And you can. Plan ahead (what food to take? what park to visit?) but don't plan too much. It can be the highlight of your trip, and an experience for your family to treasure for a lifetime.

Recommendations

✔ To save money, have a simple breakfast in your flat, buy your mid-day meal out, and fix supper back at the flat. Buy easy-to-prepare items from the neighborhood grocery in your street. You'll save money and everyone can use a late-afternoon rest at the flat after a busy afternoon of sightseeing.

✔ If you're staying at a small hotel, stoke up with the big English breakfast provided. That will allow you to eat a lighter and quicker lunch. (The kids won't let you skip it altogether.)

✔ Carry quick snacks for the kids.

✔ Eat ethnic. Be adventurous. What's the point of travelling thousands of miles just to do things the same way you do at home?

✔ Have a picnic. You can't be on the run all the time. Take a picnic lunch or supper to the Serpentine in Hyde Park or the rose garden in Regent's Park and just relax.

For the latest updates to *London for Families*,
check our page on the World Wide Web at

http://www.as.udayton.edu/com/faculty/lain/lonfam.htm

6. Getting Around

Because London grew haphazardly from an assortment of medieval villages, its streets can be tangled and confusing. Even Londoners themselves carry the book of street maps called *London A to Z*. It may be the best-selling book in the city.

On the other hand, London's public transportation system and walkability make it among the easiest large cities in the world to get around in. A map of the Underground system, a free city map, and an occasional willingness to ask for directions are all you need to get wherever you're going.

Safety

London is not like many American big cities which, sad to say, have high crime rates and sections into which even the residents fear to go. We've walked throughout central London at all hours of the day and night and never felt uncomfortable or unsafe. We like being in a place even the police seldom feel the need to carry guns.

That doesn't mean that it's OK to be foolish. A woman shouldn't walk alone after dark in deserted areas *anywhere*, whether in London or New York. Mugging is extremely rare in London but pick-pocketry is much more common than in the U.S., so valuables should be safeguarded. All the rules you've learned about safe behavior when travelling or in getting around *any* city apply here too, but with just a minimum of good sense, you're less likely to experience a problem in London than in perhaps any other of the world's major cities.

Maps

A recent check of our favorite local bookstore revealed a half-dozen maps of London available for sale at prices ranging from $4 to $8. Don't buy one! The best map is available free from the British Travel Authority. There are offices in several cities in the United States, and they'll be happy to send you maps and a wealth of other literature without charge if you ask. (Be sure to request BTA's handy little *London Guide.*) If you're in New York, Chicago, Atlanta, or Los Angeles, you can carry away pounds of free information from their walk-in offices. Here's a starting point:

British Travel Authority
551 Fifth Avenue
New York, NY 10176-0799
phone 1-800-462-2748

Each member of your family ought to carry a map. The BTA map shows all major streets in central London, major attractions, the locations of all Underground stations, and has a separate map of the Underground system.

Once you're in London, you can pick up a free map of the bus system in any Underground station. There is plenty of good local information at any of several tourist information centers, but those nice BTA London maps will cost you £1.50. Get them before you leave. They're the only maps we ever use, except for an occasional reference to a pocket-sized version of *London A to Z* we bought in London for £2.75.

Public Transportation

Don't even *think* of renting a car in London. Driving in London is next to impossible for a visitor unfamiliar with driving on the left and uncertain of the streets. It will take you much longer to get where you're going. When you get there you won't be able to find anywhere to park or, in the unlikely event that you do, the parking tariff will cost more than your hotel room. Since you're living like a local, do what most Londoners do: use public transportation.

Public transport divides the city into zones

The Underground

In England, a *subway* is an underground walkway, usually under a busy street, for pedestrians. If you're looking for an underground train, you're looking for what Londoners call the *Underground*, or more commonly, the *Tube*. London has the world's oldest underground system, and while in a few places it looks like it, it's generally clean and efficient. Stations are located in every part of the city and locals often give directions by referring to the nearest tube station.

The system consists of twelve interconnected lines and you can change from one to another free. It is seldom necessary to change lines more than once in any journey. The map of the system is extremely clear and easy to use, and if it looks to the practiced eye like a circuit diagram, that's probably because it was designed by an electrical engineer. The format makes it easy to locate your beginning and ending points and to chart your most efficient route. Everyone will catch on to the system with the first look at the map. There are clear maps of the system and of the line you're on in every car.

As you go down to the platform, make sure you get on a train going in the right direction, and follow your trip on the map. Even when stations are called out, it's often impossible to understand what the driver is saying.

Tip: *Make sure everyone in your family can use the system by having them take turns planning your route on the tube. This will give you much more comfort when they're out on their own or if you become separated.*

One of your first purchases in London should be a tube pass. While you can pay by the ride, it takes time to buy a ticket for each trip and it's much more expensive that way. You can buy Travel-Cards good for any period from one day to a month at any Underground station. If you're getting a pass for a week or more you'll need a passport-size photo. If you didn't bring one, there are automatic photo booths in all railway stations and many large tube stations. (The cost is £2.50 or so for a set of four photos.)

Fares are based on a zone system. The farther you travel, the more it costs. But if this is your first trip to London, you'll seldom leave Zone 1, Central London, so that's all you should ask for. If you leave Zone 1, you'll pay a small extra fee when you enter the station.

The tube system uses magnetic-coated tickets or fare cards. Just feed your card face-up into the slot in the turnstile and walk through. Your ticket pops up another slot as you pass through. You repeat the process when you exit the station. Simple—as long as you don't mislay your ticket en route. If you're going beyond Zone 1 (a map provided with your travelcard shows the stations in each zone) just present your card to the cashier in the station, say where you're going (ask for a "return" fare, not round-trip), pay the fee, and you'll be given a separate ticket to be used for this trip only.

Tube trains run from about 5 a.m. until shortly after midnight. Each station has a schedule of train times posted on the platform.

Buses

Red double-decker buses are as closely associated with London as Big Ben. They're not a speedy way to travel, but they're great for sightseeing and they're sometimes more convenient than the tube. You can get a map of Central London bus routes at any Underground station.

A case of low "I-queue"

Bus stops are marked clearly with the numbers of the buses that stop there. If the London Transport sign is white, all buses listed for that corner will stop there. A red sign designates a Request Stop, and you must put your arm out to signal the bus to stop.

Passengers normally queue up politely to board the bus. When you reach the driver, just show your travelcard or tube pass unless you're leaving Zone 1, in which case you'll be asked to pay a slight additional fare. If you're not sure exactly when to get off, you'll almost always finds the driver friendly and accommodating. Sit near the front and he'll let you know when it's time to get off. Otherwise, sit on the top deck for an interesting view of the passing city. Your kids will insist on it anyway, and they're right. It's fun and memorable.

There are red single-deckers owned by private bus companies and green buses which go out of central London, but you won't *really* have been to London until you've ridden upstairs on one of these stately behemoths.

Taxis

Other cities may have more modern underground systems; the buses may travel faster in less congested cities. But no city on earth has better taxis than London. The famous black taxis (which now occasionally come in other colors) are as recognizable as red double-deckers.

It takes two years of study and examination to become a London cabbie. Notice the men (or very rarely, women) on little motorbikes with a clipboard attached to the handlebars. You see them all over the city, but especially when traffic is light, like on Sunday mornings. Those are taxi driver wannabes studying the city.

Not all taxis are black anymore

Students must spend two years studying "The Knowledge," a detailed course which involves acquiring an exact geography of the city—every street, every major building, restaurant, and hotel. A passenger is able to get into any black cab, give an address, and expect to be taken there quickly by the most direct route. If you can, it's polite to give the driver a frame of reference, like "38 Cartwright Gardens, near Euston Station," but even if you don't know where you're going, your driver will.

We've never encountered an unfriendly cab driver. Most are cheerful and helpful, eager to hear about your impressions of their city and ready with advice. Fares are seldom very high, because Central London is much smaller geographically than the central areas of most major American cities. Tip the driver 10–15 percent of the fare.

Black taxis can be hailed in the street when their orange "For Hire" sign is lit, and we've never had a problem getting one,

---

Trials of a London Cabbie

A cabbie once told us that an inspector may enter his cab at any time, and will probably try to trip him up with an obscure street, or a name that might be one of several streets. For example, an inspector might ask to be taken to "150 Park." The cabbie must clarify at once which "Park" the passenger has in mind: London contains

Park Avenue (2, actually, in different parts of town)
Park Close (3 different ones)
Park Court
Park Crescent (3, all near one another)
Park End
Park Gate
Park Gardens
Park Hall
Park Hill (3 different)
Park Lane (2 different)
Park Mews
Park Place (3 different)
Park Rise
Park Rise Road
Park Road (4 different)
Parke Road
Park Row
Park Square (2 near each other)
Park Street (2 different)
The Park
Park Towers
Park View
Park Village
Park Vista
Park Walk
And that doesn't even consider city parks!

even on a rainy night (when Manhattan cabs mysteriously disappear). You can also book cabs by telephone.

Cruising

Another efficient way of getting around is often by water. River taxis run up and down the Thames and are a fun and affordable way of taking a load off your feet for a while or going from one riverside place to another. There are several piers on both sides of the river, but a nice possibility is to take a river taxi from Westminster Pier (near Big Ben) to the Tower of London. It will probably cost your family less than £15 and won't take much longer than riding the Circle Line tube train nearby. As you travel keep in mind that this is the way—by river—that the king usually travelled to the Tower: It was safer than going through the streets of a city where he was frequently unpopular.

This is also the route taken, of course, by traitors on their way to the Tower to have their heads cut off. This is a thought that might appeal to some members of your family.

In Chapter 17 we'll talk about using the river for slightly longer trips as well. Information from the River Boat Information Service is available by calling 0171-730-4812.

Near Regent's Park is an area known as Little Venice because of its many canals. England is filled with canals, and an hour's cruise on one of the long, narrow canal boats makes a relaxing break. Several companies offer economical cruises across the north of London, and most stop at the Zoo if you're going there. Two reliable companies are Jason's Trips (0171-286-3428) and London Waterbus Company (0171-482-2550).

London by Foot

By far the best way to see London, however, is to walk. London is one of the most compact of the world's major cities and with good legs and sturdy shoes you can cross the city on foot in a couple of hours. In fact, the size of Central London, where most of the tourist attractions are, isn't much different from that of our own home base of Dayton, Ohio, a city of about 180,000.

On foot you can go places too narrow for buses to venture and hidden from the eyes of passengers in the trains beneath your feet. It's cheaper than the bus or tube, and your feet operate 24 hours a day.

Don't worry about getting lost! Tube stations are everywhere, and from any tube station you can go quickly to anywhere else in the city. In the direst of straits, hail a taxi and tell the driver where you want to go. Police officers are everywhere and are invariably friendly and helpful. In fact, we *try* to get lost in London by taking the tube to an unfamiliar neighborhood and just starting to walk.

The greatest danger isn't getting lost, it's getting run over. London drivers apparently must fail a sanity test before getting a license to drive in the city. They whiz past even on congested streets. But they obey traffic lights and "zebra crossings" and that's your salvation.

Vehicles travel on the *left* in Britain, remember, so you have to look to your right when you cross the street. You'll see painted reminders to do that on almost every curb. *Never* cross in the middle of the block. Go to the corner and wait for the light, no matter how much in a hurry you are. Zebra crossings are cross-walks with wide black-and-white stripes leading across the street

Look for the zebra and pelican crossings

and a flashing yellow light at each end. Drivers are required to stop whenever a pedestrian is in the crossing and they always do. But give them enough time to see you. The car coming at you is going too fast (count on it!) and needs time to stop. Teach your children not to act like children in crossing the street. It's the most dangerous thing in England.

When you walk you discover the most surprising things. Some of our favorite walking-around discoveries include:

- two or three colorful festivals
- an open-air market not listed in any guidebook we've ever seen
- lovely, tranquil neighborhood parks
- unusual monuments to people both familiar and forgotten
- fragments of ruins of the 2,000-year-old Roman wall
- the site of an old palace of Henry VIII
- an ancient and architecturally unique pub
- and dozens of other special places.

Walking through London gives you a chance to look closely at buildings and unusual street furniture like lampposts and statues, to watch the buskers trying to entertain you for a couple of bob, to read the blue plaques on the fronts of buildings to discover their famous former inhabitants, and to begin to feel a part of this historic city. You'll enjoy the window shopping and the stunning unexpected view when you turn a corner and suddenly the great dome of St. Paul's lies ahead. Go to London not only to visit the tourist attractions, but to learn about the culture and life of the place. That's something your children will be influenced by long after the specific details of the Abbey or the Tower have dimmed in their memories. That's why you take a family on a vacation like this: Not merely to *see* a place, but to *experience* it.

There are organized walking tours, too. You'll probably find a brochure at your hotel or at any tourist information booth for Original London Walks and one or two other companies. These walks, which last about two hours and cost about £5 per person (student discounts available), have themes like *Shakespeare and*

Dickens or the popular *Jack the Ripper Walk*. They cover in detail a part of London associated with the theme and are always led by extremely knowledgeable, entertaining guides, who will take you places you'd never have found on your own and tell you stories you'd never have got from the guidebooks. They begin at an Underground station and end near another, making travel to and from the walks easy and convenient.

An excellent book to take along would be *American Walks in London*. The ten walks in this book (each starting and ending at a tube stop) will take you to all London's most famous sights as well as to places you never knew existed. See where Benjamin Franklin worked as a printer in a church over eight centuries old, where Whistler painted *that* portrait of his mother, where Teddy Roosevelt got married, where FDR spent his honeymoon. If your family enjoys walking and you *really* want to get off the beaten track, *The Independent Walker's Guide to Great Britain* is the book to buy before you go. It takes you on thirty-five enchanting walks and allows you to explore England, Scotland, and Wales as a walker, and truly see Great Britain through the back door.

Getting Oriented

If this is your first time in London, you might want to take a general tour soon after you arrive to give you and your family a general feel for the city. There are several good ways to do that.

Bus Tours

There are numerous bus tours of London, usually in open-topped double-deckers, which are ideal on dry days. The commentary is informative, if a little too practiced sometimes, but they all give you a good overview of the major sights and where they sit in relation to each other. Best bets may be the tours run by London Transport and by the Big Bus Company. Bus tours are pricey but will give you the highlights quickly.

Getting Around

The LT tour leaves every 20 to 30 minutes from Victoria Station, Piccadilly Circus, Marble Arch, and the Baker Street Underground. Tours last about 90 minutes and cost about £10 for adults and £5 for children.

The Big Bus tours leave from Marble Arch, Victoria Station, and in front of the Ritz and Royal Westminster hotels. Their "Stopper Tours" allow you to get on and off the bus as you wish at any of fourteen different attractions around the city. Tickets are good for 24 hours and cost about £12 for adults and £6 for children. Buses leave about every half-hour.

By Taxi

A cheaper but more superficial tour might simply be to tell your taxi driver to drive you past some of the sights on your way to your lodgings. His commentary won't be as witty or complete as the one you'll get on the bus, but he'll be happy to show you around the neighborhood. He'll probably ask you how extensive a tour you want, but £15 should get you the Westminster and Soho areas, or whatever comparably-sized areas are near to where you're staying.

The Lains' Guided Walking Tour of Central London

You won't cover as much ground as you will on the bus, but if you'd like to walk along with us for a couple of pages, we'll take you on a quick tour of the West End on foot, the same tour Larry gives the American college students he sometimes takes to London. You can walk this route in well under two hours, or it could take much longer if you enter some of the attractions today, stop to eat, and so on. There's no need to do it all at once, of course. The walk goes within a block of seven tube stations, so you can opt out at any time. But it's a good way to start your trip because the walk will take you past some of the most important sights in London and give you a good idea of just how compact historic London really is.

So grab your camera, tighten the laces on your shoes, and let's go.

Piccadilly Circus: This is a convenient starting place, so take the tube (Piccadilly or Bakerloo lines) to the "Times Square of London" and we'll begin. Seven major streets converge here. The statue of Eros is no longer in the center of the intersection, but crossing the street is an adventure. Use the pedestrian subways to get to the southwest corner of the intersection of Piccadilly and Regent Street. If you haven't eaten for a while there's plenty of opportunity to stoke up before you begin. There's a Garfunkel's restaurant, a moderately-priced family restaurant at the intersection, and several other inexpensive places within your gaze.

Now we'll walk down *Piccadilly* past a wide variety of shops and restaurants. Across the street is the very exclusive and expensive Burlington Arcade, with some of the best window shopping in London. But no whistling or running in the Arcade or a frock-coated beadle may ask you to leave.

We go by the Ritz Hotel and find a large park on our left. This is *Green Park*, one of the Royal Parks, former hunting preserves of the King. Turn left and take a walk through this cool and lovely green space. At the opposite end of the park you'll find a great building set at the end of a broad avenue. Welcome to *Buckingham Palace*.

If you've come in the morning there will be a large crowd waiting for the Changing of the Guard, but at other times of the day it's fairly quiet here. Across from the main gate is a statue of Queen Victoria, the first monarch to make this her home.

Walk past the front gate of the Palace. If the flag is flying atop the building, it means the Queen is in residence. Perhaps as you pass she'll step out onto the balcony and say to herself, "What a lovely American family that is!" and then holler down for you to come in and join her at tea. But if that doesn't happen, bear to the left after you pass the Palace down the short *Spur Road* to *Birdcage Walk*. Turn left and enjoy the stroll along Birdcage Walk, with St. James's Park, another of the Royal Parks, on your left and elegant 18th- and 19th-century buildings on your right. Or walk through the park in the same direction instead.

When you come to the end of St. James's Park, turn right on *Storey's Gate*. You'll pass the huge Methodist Central Hall, then

Big Ben and Call Box: Enduring images of London

suddenly find yourself staring into the face of the holiest and most important church in all England: *Westminster Abbey*, the burial place of kings and saints. And now, behind the Abbey, stand the *Houses of Parliament* and the great tower of *Big Ben*. Chapter 13 goes into more detail about these magnificent buildings.

As you bear to the left and pass the Abbey on your right, you'll see a smaller church tucked next to it. This is St. Margaret's Church, an important church in its own right but almost unknown to Americans. Its place in history is well established by the fact that for centuries, in times of crisis, Parliament has met here for prayer, and that this was where such luminaries as John Milton and Winston Churchill were married.

When you reach the street separating the Abbey from Parliament, turn left. You'll walk past *Parliament Square* with its statue of Churchill, and proceed straight up *Parliament Street*, which soon changes its name to *Whitehall*. Here is the seat of British government.

Walk up the left side of the street. In the middle of Whitehall stands a sober monument called the *Cenotaph*, a memorial to British war dead. Just past the Cenotaph you'll find an iron gate on your left, with two police constables on duty. You're at the entrance to *Downing Street*, and just down the way you'll see *No. 10*, the residence of the British Prime Minister and the equivalent of the White House in the United States. The police officers won't let you any closer but they always seem ready for a cheery chat.

Just a bit further on, across the street, is *Banqueting House*, built in 1622 as part of the royal palace complex. From a window in this building in 1648, King Charles II stepped onto a scaffold for his execution during the English Civil War. A little further yet, on your side of the street, is the *Horse Guards Parade*, with a brilliantly-uniformed soldier standing silent guard. Children from everywhere in the world pet the horse's nose and have a picture taken standing beside the guard. They're quite tame—the horse, that is, although the guard probably is too, when he's off duty.

When you come to the top of Whitehall you're at the very hub of London—*Trafalgar Square*, a vast public plaza with the memorial column to Lord Nelson at its heart. This is a good place to sit down and rest your feet for a few minutes.

Trafalgar Square is Pigeon Central. They're uncountable! Londoners hate them the same way Floridians hate seagulls; they're obnoxious and messy. But the tourists love them and for 20p the kids can buy seed to feed them. Stand still in the middle of the square and you'll soon be covered with them.

Kids' other favorite activity here is to climb the lions for a photograph. Go ahead. Don't be afraid to act like a tourist here. Everybody you see is a tourist. There's probably not a native within shouting distance.

Across the square is the *National Gallery*, one of the world's important art museums with the spire of *St. Martin-in-the-Fields*

Relaxing at Trafalgar Square near St. Martin-in-the-Fields Church

Church to the right. Invisible behind the National Gallery is the *National Portrait Gallery*, home to the original paintings of kings and queens we've seen in so many history books. Behind you and off to the left is the *Admiralty Arch*. Behind you and to the right is the Strand, once the chief river's edge street, and *Charing Cross Station*. Charing Cross is properly the center of London, since all streets and directions are figured from here.

When your feet are rested, walk along the right side of the National Gallery and cross the street (St. Martin's Lane) in front of the National Portrait Gallery. Now you're in the theatre district. Stroll up St. Martin's Lane to *Garrick Street*, named for the great

Shakespearean actor, soaking up the edge of theatreland, and turn right. When you get to *King Street*, turn left. A few blocks later and you're in the famous *Covent Garden*.

This is another place you could spend your entire trip, a bustling, cheery marketplace with something happening every minute. Good bargains can be found in the craft and antiques markets here, and buskers, London's street entertainers, perform non-stop. The Punch and Judy pub attracts crowds to its balcony to refresh themselves and watch the shows go on below, and there are dozens of places within a one-minute walk to get anything from a quick snack to an elegant £100 meal. Centerpiece of the plaza is St. Paul's Church (*not* St. Paul's Cathedral), known as "The Actor's Church" because of its centuries-old association with the theatre. A plaque on the church marks the spot of the first-known Punch and Judy puppet play. The church will be off to your right as you enter the plaza from King Street.

If the plaza looks familiar it's probably because you remember it from the movie *My Fair Lady*. Many of the scenes were filmed right here.

Stay, shop, watch, and enjoy as long as you like, then leave the plaza by continuing up King Street to *James Street*, about halfway along the market building. Turn left up James St. and a block later, at the Covent Garden Underground station, you've reached *Long Acre*. Turn left here and go back to St. Martin's Lane.

We have several choices here, all of them excellent. There are dozens of quaint little shops all around you selling some real bargains . . . and some *really* overpriced merchandise. But we'll shop later. Herd your troop back across the street. The Underground station you're in front of now is Leicester Square (pronounce it *Lester*). If we turn right, we go up *Charing Cross Road*, with its dozens of second-hand bookshops. The bibliophiles in your family will surely want to return for shopping. But let's continue straight ahead into busy *Leicester Square* itself. You really feel in the heart of the theatre district now as you pass movie theatres and ticket agencies (mostly selling for a high price tickets you could buy at the box office for less). As you approach the crowded park you'll probably see a long queue of people. They're waiting at the *Half-Price Ticket Booth*. The theatres release unsold seats on the day of performance to this location to sell for half price, plus a small service charge. Few of the top shows like *Cats* or *Phantom* are available here, but excellent tickets to the vast majority of London shows can be bought here and it's one of the best buys in town.

A block or so past Leicester Square, *Wardour Street* runs off to the right. Following it for two blocks will put you into the midst of London's *Chinatown*. Its main street, *Gerrard Street*, is a colorful pedestrian thoroughfare off to the right where you might spend fifteen minutes soaking up the colorful neighborhood.

Return to Wardour Street and follow it another block until you reach *Shaftesbury Avenue*. Turn left here and a short walk will take you right back to Piccadilly Circus, the starting point of our tour.

We haven't seen everything, of course. There's St. Paul's Cathedral, the Tower, the Thames! But this walk through the West End is a wonderful introduction to some of the exciting sights and sites of the city, and should whet everyone's appetite for what will come.

Recommendations

✔ Get free maps and literature by calling the BTA's toll-free number before you leave home.

✔ Make a TravelCard or tube pass one of your first purchases when you arrive.

✔ Sample all of London's transportation options, but most of all, walk. It's more fun, often just as fast, and will let you see things you'd have missed otherwise.

7. Money Matters

H andling money in England is no more complicated than it is at home. You'll have to get used to the look and feel of their currency, and you'll have to make some decisions about how you want to handle the transactions of converting your own currency into pounds, but we'll give you all the information you need to thrive in the next few pages. We'll describe the currency system in Britain, talk about how much money to take, what form to take it in, and give you some tips on how to carry your money.

The British Currency System

For centuries, and up until about a generation ago, the system of English money was almost incomprehensible to foreigners. The British used an ancient monetary system that involved twelve pence (pennies) to the shilling and twenty shillings to the pound, with a bewildering assortment of other denominations like farthings, crowns, and guineas thrown in for good measure. Fortunately for us tourists, those days are gone and seem just as puzzling to younger British as they do to us. Like nearly all the rest of the world's monetary systems, the British pound is now based on a simple decimal system. A few of the old words survive, but even they are seldom used any more.

The basic unit of British money is the *pound sterling*, usually just called the pound or, occasionally, referred to as sterling (as in "I'd like to convert $100 U.S. into sterling, please."). Stick with "pounds" and you'll never go astray. The pound sign (£) is nothing more than a handwritten capital "L" with a stroke through it. (We know, it doesn't make sense to use an "L" as an abbreviation for "pounds." But then, it doesn't make a lot of sense to use an "S" with a stroke to abbreviate "dollars" either.)

They call them pounds *for a reason*

The pound consists of 100 pennies called *pence*, which is actually abbreviated with a lower case "*p*" and is pronounced the same way. So you'd say something like "The newspaper costs 20p," pronouncing the price as "*twenty pee.*"

That's all there is to it; you've mastered the British monetary system! Now all you have to do is recognize the denominations. And that's something you'll catch on to with one day's practice.

Paper Currency

The bits of currency—folding money—are called *notes* rather than bills, so you may have a £5 note in your pocket instead of a $5 bill.

It's easier to distinguish denominations of currency in Britain because as a rule the more a note is worth, the larger it is. A £5 note (often called a "fiver") is the smallest folding money made, both in value and in size; £10 notes are larger, and most £20 notes are bigger still. If you have a £50 note it will probably stick up out of your wallet and get tattered around the edge if you can avoid spending it for a few days. We don't have enough money to have ever encountered larger notes, but if the pattern holds, you could probably use them for tablecloths. In recent years, however, the Bank of England has begun issuing currency in smaller sizes, so you might well have two £20 notes of different sizes in your wallet.

When you give a note to a merchant, don't be surprised if he or she holds it quickly up to the light. British notes incorporate two safeguards to discourage counterfeiting. They have a metallic strip running through them vertically, and they also have an unprinted oval on the front in which you can see a picture of the Queen when you hold it to the light. Both are impossible to duplicate on even very sophisticated color copying machines that have made counterfeiting much easier than it was years ago.

Coinage

The British use seven coins, and all are in common circulation, unlike the U.S., where two of the six coins—the half dollar and the dollar—are so rare as to create excitement when you get one in change. Here's the lineup:

Denomination	Description
1p	penny, similar to an American penny
2p	tuppence, same color as a penny, much larger
5p	silver-colored, looks like a dime; still occasionally called a shilling or a "bob"
10p	silver-colored, almost the size of the tuppence, round in shape

20p	silver-colored, slightly larger than the penny, but seven-sided
50p	largest of the silver coins, but is seven-sided
£1	a little larger than a penny but brass color, very thick and rather heavy.

On your first day in Britain you'll count your coins carefully whenever you pay or receive change. By the third day using the new coins will be automatic and something you do with barely a glance.

Should You Take British Pounds or Your Own Currency?

Even experienced travellers debate this question. Some claim that exchange rates are better in Britain, so they carry their own money on vacation and change it into British currency as they need it. Others contend that exchange rates are usually better at home and that currency conversion is best done at home, both for the price and for the convenience. We weigh in with the latter group.

We've talked to travellers returning from Britain within days of our leaving for a trip, and in every case the exchange rate we got at home was better than the one they'd received just days earlier in Britain. We're convinced that we get a better deal at home. The convenience factor is important, too. If all our money is in pounds when we get to Britain, we can start our vacation immediately. We don't have to line up at the bank in the airport to get money for the train or the airbus; we just collect our baggage and we're ready to go. That's what we recommend. We normally have our money in hand at least a week, sometimes much longer, before we leave.

Currency Exchange

We keep an eye on the exchange rates published in the newspaper. The paper we usually read publishes them daily on the same page as the stock tables, but almost all large newspapers publish them at least weekly, often in the Sunday travel section. Since about 1993, the exchange rate in the United States has held fairly steady at about \$1.60 to \$1.65 per British pound, so timing hasn't been especially important lately. But as recently as 1992 values were fluctuating wildly. In less than two months time the price of a pound rose from \$1.78 to \$2.12, which means that if you were planning to buy £1,000 for a trip, the money could have cost you anywhere between \$1,780 and \$2,120, a difference of \$340. We knew we were going to England that summer and bought our money early, as soon as we saw the prices start to shoot up. But there's always an element of risk, just like with the stock market. Maybe the price will improve if you wait. Honestly, though, it seldom makes as big a difference as it did in that particular year. Lately, the fluctuation over the course of a year hasn't been more than about 10 cents. Just keep an eye on it.

Three Types of Money

You can carry three types of money, and a mixture of all three is the best bet: *cash, travellers cheques,* and *credit cards.* Don't bring your checkbook; personal checks will not be honored abroad, except at American Express offices which will cash small personal checks for members.

We recommend that you use a mixture of all three forms of payment. Most businesses will prefer to be paid in cash, and many places abroad don't like to take travellers cheques. While the use of credit cards has become common in Europe, there are still some places like some small hotels and B&Bs, as well as some merchants, who don't take them. But at the very least, have enough British cash with you when you arrive to get you through the expenses of your first day—transportation from the airport, meals, tube passes, and incidentals.

Let's look at the three types of money you'll be carrying.

Cash

Banks will change almost any currency

Any bank can get foreign currency for you. Larger banks in sizable cities may even have a foreign currency department; smaller banks may have to order it for you and that can take a few days. Also, different banks may offer slightly different exchange rates. When you're ready to get money for your trip, telephone two or three banks and ask about their rates and availability. You'll probably have to pay American cash for foreign currency, although if you buy it from the place you normally bank, they should take a check.

We suggest you carry enough cash for a day or two, and that you carry most of the rest of your funds in travellers cheques. However, children should be allowed to carry their own money, if they're old enough to do so at home. That way they know how much they have left of their allotted amount and can learn to plan ahead. If your stay will be a lengthy one, you may prefer to give them their money in weekly increments.

We normally carry almost no American money. You can't spend it in England any more easily than you can spend British pounds in Ohio, so we take just enough for snacks and incidentals during airport layovers. But if you do have dollars you need to convert to pounds while you're in Britain, *don't do it at your hotel!* This is surely the worst place in England to buy money. The exchange rate will be *much* worse than anywhere else you're likely to try; you pay dearly for convenience.

A slightly better choice are the Bureaux de Change you'll see all over London. They handle large quantities of many world currencies, and their exchange rates are posted clearly. Most branches of the bigger travel agencies, like Thomas Cook, will also change money. But beware: the best exchange rate does not always mean the best deal, because service charges and percentage commission may differ from one place to another. Banks may be your best bet, though. Most of them post their rates, too, so if you plan to change a substantial amount of money, spend a little time shopping around for the best deal. Banks in heavy tourist areas like Covent Garden will probably give a somewhat less favorable exchange rate than other branches of the same bank elsewhere in town.

You will normally be asked for your passport when you change money.

Travellers Cheques

Carry most of your money in travellers cheques. They can be replaced if they're lost or stolen, and that safety provides for great peace of mind when you have all your vacation funds with you.

Unlike the custom in North America, however, travellers cheques are not always easy to spend directly. Many places won't take them at all, some do so only grudgingly, or after adding a small service charge. The best thing to do with travellers cheques is to exchange them at a bank for two or three days worth of cash as you need it.

We recommend taking your travellers cheques in pound de-

> *Tip:* If you're a member of the American Automobile Association (AAA) you can get American Express travellers cheques in pounds for no service fee. Banks usually charge a fee of 1% of the purchase.

nominations, not in dollars or other currencies. Again, we have found the most favorable exchange rates at home, not abroad, and many places in Britain will charge a £1–2 service fee to exchange foreign-denomination cheques. If you buy your cheques at home in pounds, you're locking in the exchange rate, in case it should become less favorable later on. Your bank can sell you cheques in pound denominations.

Most banks in Britain will convert your travellers cheques into cash at no charge, but a few will charge a £1–2 service fee. Ask. Bureaux de Change usually also charge a small fee. We have never been charged at Lloyd's or Barclays banks. American Express offices will also exchange American Express travellers cheques in pounds for cash at no charge.

Credit Cards

Credit cards are now widely accepted in Britain, although you'll find more places that don't take them than you will in North America. Some other places, especially smaller hotels, occasionally add a surcharge of five to ten percent for card users. Nevertheless, most of the time a credit card is a convenient source of emergency money, or a convenient alternative to paying cash for unexpected large purchases.

Where credit cards are accepted, most American cards are recognized. Visa, Mastercard, and American Express are commonly accepted, and Discover, Carte Blanche, and Diner's Club are not uncommon. Places that accept the British Access or Barclaycard will usually accept Visa and Mastercard, but it's a good idea to check before making a purchase. Eurocard and JCB are also normally well received.

The greatest danger of a credit card is the same as it is at home: It's easy to rack up lots of bills in a short time without noticing. But if you're not inclined to max out your card at home, you probably won't abroad, either. Good spending habits don't stop at the border.

One other danger is that you never know exactly what you're paying for something until you get the bill. Currency conversions are based on the exchange rate on the day the charge is posted to your account. The difference between what you expect and what you get probably won't be great, but it's worth keeping in mind. If you're thinking about an exchange rate of $1.60 per British pound (and so expecting the £100 Wedgewood tea set to cost $160) you might find that by the time the charge was posted the exchange rate had risen to £1 = $1.65 (meaning the tea set cost you an extra $5).

On the other hand, the exchange rate might go down, *saving* you money. Over a period of time, it'll probably even out. Actually, the true exchange rate you'll be charged is probably two or three percent better than you could get from your bank at home because your card will be charged at the *bank* rate, which is cheaper than the consumer rate.

ATMs in Britain

That brings up one other possibility for obtaining money: using the Automatic Teller Machine (ATM) at a British bank.

Many travellers maintain that this is the best and cheapest way of obtaining foreign currency. The bank rate for currency conversion is cheaper than the over-the-counter consumer rate, and the cheaper bank rate is what you're charged when you use an ATM. That can save you two or three percent over what you'd be charged at home—$20 or $30 per $1,000 of currency purchases.

We've used ATMs abroad for emergency cash, but have decided that it's better to take with us what we expect to need. Larry once spent over an hour on a Sunday morning looking for an ATM that would take his bank card. He found two or three but they were locked behind doors that could only be opened by customers of a particular bank. He finally got his money because of the kindness of a bank customer who opened the door for him.

Make sure you have a 4-digit PIN number, and be certain it's given in *numbers*, not in letters, because that's what European ATM machines will expect. Otherwise the machines work just as they do at home and will provide cash advances up to the limit of your credit and the regulations of the card company.

How Much Money to Take

If you've peeked ahead at the budget worksheet in Chapter 20, you've seen that we recommend budgeting on the high side and taking ten percent more money than you expect to spend. We've come home from every trip we've ever taken with money left over because we're pretty conservative financially (call it *cheap* if you like) and we'd rather take too much than not enough. A few times we've actually made a bit of money because the exchange rate was higher when we disposed of our money after returning home than it was when we bought it before we left. We carry most of our money in travellers cheques, seldom starting out with more than about £100 in cash, except for once when the manager of the flat we were renting stipulated that the rent had to be paid on arrival in cash. That's not an uncommon requirement. So our recommendation: Rely mostly on cash and travellers cheques, because they lock in your exchange rate and make it easy for you to keep track of how much you're spending. Carry a credit card or two for emergencies or for unexpected large purchases, and you'll do just fine.

Carrying Your Money

The worst thing about carrying large amounts of money is how nervous it makes you feel. The last thing you want to have happen is to lose your wallet or purse, or maybe worse, fall victim to a pickpocket. Be warned that while outright mugging is rare in Europe, pickpocketry is much more common than in North America, so you should carry your money cautiously. Men, carry your wallet in your side pocket, not in the back; women, keep your purses close to your body, and with the handle over your shoulder, if possible, not swinging from your hand. Don't put your valuables in a "fanny pack" strapped around your waist, because they're easy to slice off in a crowd. (By the way, what North Americans call a "fanny pack" is called a *bum bag* in Britain, where the word "fanny" is offensive and rude.)

The very best advice we can give, though, is to invest in a money belt. This is a zippered pouch that fastens around your waist under your slacks or skirt. It's impossible to pickpocket unless the thief can undress you without your noticing, and it will hold all your money except what you need for the day. You should never leave your money in your hotel room, or even your flat really, but with money belts on both Mom and Dad, the entire family treasury can be carried comfortably and invisibly. Take only what money you expect to need for the day's activities, and if you run short, 30 seconds in a rest room is plenty of time to retrieve a little extra cash. A money belt will cost less than a family meal at a fast-food restaurant, and will help ensure that there is plenty of money for those family meals.

If it's more comfortable for you, buy a pouch that goes around your neck under your shirt or blouse. Either way, after the first day you won't even notice you're wearing it, but you have the security of knowing your vacation funds are safe from loss or theft.

An Expense Diary

Here is one final money tip: In chapter three we suggested that you keep a diary or journal of your trip as a memento. Consider writing down all your expenses as part of the diary. We don't necessarily mean small purchases like newspapers and ice cream bars, but meals, souvenirs, tickets, and so on. It's a technique that's guaranteed to help you stay on budget because you're aware of exactly what you're spending. Looking back at those expense journals years later also helps to bring back memories of the trip—*"Oh, yes, I remember the haloumi I had at Andrea's Restaurant that day. Delicious!"*

An expense diary once had one other very nice benefit. Returning to the United States after more than three weeks in England several years ago, we were dismayed in passing through customs to hear one inspector say to another, "We haven't checked anyone from this flight yet. I guess we'd better. Oh, sir . . ."—and tapped Larry on the shoulder. Larry said that he was willing to let them check his bags, but that before he did, they could see for themselves exactly what he was bringing back, and produced his diary from his carry-on. Every purchase was recorded by date, item, and amount. "Wow!" the inspector said, "I've never seen anybody with such good records." He glanced at the diary and waved us through, asking to see just one item.

Recommendations

✔ Convert your money into pounds before you leave home.

✔ Carry most of your money in travellers cheques, with enough cash to get you through your first day or two in London.

✔ Bring along a credit card or two for emergency cash or major purchases.

✔ Buy and use a money belt or neck pouch for your money reserves.

8. *Living Like a Local*

In Chapter 4 we talked about the value of "living like a local." It's one of the main reasons, other than cost, that we urge you to forego the big hotels. In an American-style hotel you're insulated from the culture of the place you're visiting. If that's what you want, why travel?

One week in London, even one month, will not make you feel like a local. You're still rooted in another place. But if you try to experience as much as possible the vibrant life of the city as the locals do, you'll come home with stories and experiences that go well beyond the almost identical photographs most tourists bring home. In the next few pages we'll present a brief survival kit that offers a short course on several aspects of living in London.

Basics of Daily Life

In many respects, life in a big city is much the same everywhere. People shop, eat, go from one place to another, read newspapers, watch TV, go to the park, and so on. It's not the things people do that are different as you go from place to place, it's the *way* they do them. The differences are in the little things, not in the big things.

The most valuable advice anyone can give you about fitting into the culture of another country is: *Relax!* Accept the fact that you *will* make mistakes, that people *will* realize that you're a tourist, that somewhere along the line you *will* do something mildly embarrassing, and that you will *not* create an international incident. If you can accept those things and just relax, you'll be much more comfortable, and you'll make the people around you more comfortable, too.

Imagine a Londoner coming for a visit to your home town. He probably wouldn't know the little day-to-day conventions that you take for granted, he'd make mistakes, maybe say things that sounded naive or silly. As long as he was polite and good humored, didn't act arrogantly as though *you* were wrong for not doing things *his* way in your own country, you'd gladly overlook the mistakes he made and you'd try to make him feel welcome. That's exactly what you can expect when you visit London.

Talk this idea over with your children. One reason you're taking this trip is so they can experience another culture. They'll find it different from their own in perplexing and amusing ways. But they need to understand that the way Americans do things isn't necessarily the *right* way. It's just *our* way. When you're a guest in someone else's country, you abide by your host's way of doing things, just as you do when you're a guest in somebody else's home. You're on your best behavior, you don't criticize, you ask about what you don't understand, and maybe you learn something valuable.

Shopping

London is like large cities all over the world, where many people don't drive any more than they can help because of the terrible traffic congestion. In fact, many people don't even own cars and rely on public transportation exclusively. That means they don't go to the supermarket and come home with a trunk filled with groceries . . . No trunks!

Everyday life in a city like London means buying fewer groceries and shopping more often. You'll see few large supermarkets but you'll find small grocery stores in every neighborhood. If you're

A colorful food market in Chinatown

staying in a flat, you're certain to begin shopping the London way, buying for just a few days at a time. Refrigerators and pantry space are smaller in your flat than you're probably used to at home, so storing two weeks' worth of food for a family would be difficult.

On your first London afternoon pick up the staples you're going to need for the week, and get meat, dairy products, and produce as you need them. Don't be surprised to find an outdoor fruit and vegetable market within a few blocks of your house. In Chapter 3 we suggested you pack a fold-up shopping bag or string bag. Spontaneous shopping, often in small quantities, is one good reason for this. Some stores used to charge a penny or two for a bag to carry your purchases home in, but this is becoming less common. Many will still expect you to pack up your own groceries, however.

Most foods are sold in metric measures. A litre is just a little larger that a quart, and a kilogram (1000 grams) is a bit over two pounds. It may take you a little longer to get used to this than the money system, but no one is likely to try to cheat you. Clothing sizes are different here, too, so you will want to try things on before buying.

When we go into retail stores in the United States, we're accustomed to having a clerk approach us with a polite "May I help you?" That's much less likely to happen in England, where clerks will normally wait for customers to approach them. They're not trying to be cold, unfriendly, or unhelpful, but it's just a manifestation of British reserve, the desire not to intrude or press oneself on someone. If you ask for a clerk's help you'll get thorough and efficient service, although perhaps without the artificial cheerfulness of an American clerk.

Most things you buy will be assessed a Value Added Tax (called VAT), a sort of sales tax. This tax, currently at 17.5 percent, is almost always *included* in the price. Prices for those few items sold net of VAT will be marked "Exclusive of VAT," in which case the tax will be added.

It is often possible to get a refund of the VAT for items you take out of the country when you leave, but frankly unless you've purchased large and expensive items like a set of china or a new camera, it's probably not worth the trouble. It involves filling out a form for each purchase with the merchant (some may have a minimum purchase requirement of as much as £50 for this), standing in line to get the paperwork processed when you leave the country, and waiting for a check, issued in British pounds, to be sent to your home and which your bank will charge a sizable fee to cash. Keep the refund in mind in case you do make substantial purchases, however.

Laundry

There's bound to be a laundromat nearby

You will find few differences in England from what you're used to at coin-operated launderettes at home. You'll probably pay more than £2 to wash and dry a load of laundry. The washer will be at least £1, and 20p in the dryer won't buy more than five minutes of heat. Some laundries might have spin dryers for which there is little or no charge; that's like putting your clothes through an extra spin cycle, getting them a bit drier before you put them in the heated dryer. Rely as much as possible on quick-dry, wrinkle-free fabrics, get an extra wearing out of what you can, and wash out some items in the sink to minimize the need to go to the launderette. For lugging clothes back and forth to the launderette, pack a laundry bag. It's a lot lighter than a suitcase.

The Media

Britain has more than a dozen daily newspapers, and something to suit every taste. Generally speaking, the full-size broadsheets like the *Times* and the *Guardian* are the most respectable papers. A few tabloids like the *Daily Express* and the *Evening Standard* (the only afternoon paper) also do a generally good, unbiased job of reporting the news. But other tabs like the *Sun*, the *Daily Star*, and the *Daily Mirror* are much more sensational than even the most outrageous daily newspapers in the United States. Several still feature large doses of sex and nudity (most often on page 3, if you're looking) and they're packed with splashy headlines and superficial stories. They're also the largest-selling English-language daily newspapers in the world.

Apart from the *Evening Standard*, these are national papers, and everybody reads a newspaper or two every day. You may not be in England long enough to become well versed on their local issues, but it's interesting and educational for the whole family to look at the way the British view world issues, or what they have to say about what's happening in America. Encourage the kids to bring a couple of issues home. They'll make good school reports, conversation pieces, and souvenirs. The London papers represent a different sort of journalism and reflect a very different view of the world than the hometown daily we're used to.

Television in Britain is an experience unto itself

Television in Britain is an odd mix. High quality drama worthy of PBS may be followed by something as silly and sexy as Benny Hill. Serious documentaries are more common than at home, and so are nudity and risque language. You'll see American programs you're used to watching, and American programs that flopped at home but became popular here.

You will find fewer channels than you're probably used to. There are just five regular over-the-air channels in England. Two of them are operated by the BBC and three are independent commercial stations. Cable is still uncommon, but many places have added satellite TV packages. You may find CNN as part of such a package, and more stations carrying American reruns, but you'll see many sports you're not used to watching, too. Cricket and billiards (called "snooker") are popular television fare here.

Many gift shops sell video tours of museums and palaces. If you're tempted to buy one as a souvenir, check the package carefully. In England, television broadcasting is on what's called the PAL system, while in the U.S. and Canada, the NTSC system is used. What that means to you is that the tapes from one system won't play on televisions that use the other system. If you buy a British videotape, it may cost you more than you paid for it originally to get it converted for use on an American TV.

The BBC also operates five radio services, encompassing classical music, popular music, news, talk-drama-sports, and educational programming. In addition there are many independent stations. Your radio will work fine in England, but those with analog tuning will do better than those with digital tuning because their stations are spaced closer together than ours, and most inexpensive American digital radios are factory set to pick up stations only in increments of 10 megaHertz. That means that in the U.S. you might find a radio station at 630 or 640 AM, but in England there might be a station at 638, which your radio wouldn't tune in sharply.

Telephone

Almost as recognizable to tourists as the red double-decker buses are the boxy red telephone booths. British Telecom began phasing them out a few years ago in favor of cheaper and more modern public phones, but users raised such a cry of outrage that some have remained in place as reminders of the old days.

There are actually two major competing telephone companies in Britain, British Telecom and Mercury, and they have their own phone booths. The phones for both companies are simple to use and service is generally good.

Many public phones are still coin operated, and a local call costs

10p. If you're talking on the phone and hear a rapid pipping sound, you're being warned that your time has almost expired and you need to put in more money or you'll be disconnected.

More often these days, public phones work with a phonecard system. A phonecard looks much like a credit card and is sold by almost every newsagent, and by other merchants as well, in London. In buying a phonecard, you're really paying for your calls in advance. You can buy them in denominations of £2, £5, £10, and £20, which give you the equivalent of 20, 50, 100, and 200 basic units.

You slide the card into the slot and make your call. A counter on the telephone tells you how many units remain on the card. If your card is used up before your call is finished, a button on the phone will release your card and allow you to insert another one.

Dialing is just like home, but when the phone on the other end rings, you hear pairs of short rings instead of one long ring as you do at home. The busy signal is a rapid beeping sound.

Calling home is expensive, but you can use major phone charge cards like MCI, Sprint, and AT&T just as you do at home. Call your carrier for the British telephone number to use for access. An increasing number of telephones also take American Express, Visa, MasterCard, Discover, and other credit cards. Instructions are posted and are quite simple.

Calls to the United States begin with 00 (the international dialing code) followed by a 1 (the code for the U.S.), followed by the area code and phone number. Calls go through quickly and are usually very clear.

Medical Matters

Emergencies, even for visitors, are covered by Britain's National Health Service, but if you seek other medical or dental care, you'll be expected to pay cash. Check with your own health insurance company for the way your plan covers your family. Typically you'll be reimbursed all or most of what you spend, but details vary greatly.

You'll find few drugstores in London, but don't worry—a chemist's shop is the same thing. The most common chain is probably Boots. A "dispensing chemist" is a drugstore that fills prescriptions. You'll find everything in a chemist's shop that you will in a drugstore back home, but names may be different. To find band-aids for your blisters, for example, you may have to ask for "sticking plasters."

As we said in Chapter 3, if you take prescription medication, bring your medicine with you in the original bottle from your pharmacy, and bring a written copy of your prescription, using the generic name, not the brand name, for the drugs you take.

It's rare to find a chemist open late at night, but the police have a list should it be necessary.

Time, Temperature, and Distance

What could be different about telling time? More than you'd think. While people will still refer to 3 p.m. as "3 o'clock" when they're speaking, when it's written down you'll often see it as 15.00. Written times are usually given on a 24-hour clock, something you'll get used to seeing on train schedules, theatre listings, and closing times. Also note that there's a period, not a colon in the time, so it's 15.00, not 15:00. It's easy enough to catch on to; just subtract twelve from all hours 13 or greater.

You may occasionally encounter a little different phrasing if you ask someone the time. If you've left your watch at the flat and ask a passerby for the time, you might hear something like "It's half ten, mate." Most places that will mean half an hour past ten o'clock, or 10:30 (or maybe 22.30). But there are places where the local dialect would interpret a statement like that to mean half an hour *before* ten, or 9:30.

Don't be startled to hear that the predicted high temperature for the first day of your London vacation in June is 20 degrees. The celsius system (also called centigrade) is usually used in Britain, just as it is almost everywhere else in the world. Don't bother with a mathematical formula for converting one to the other. Start at 0 degrees celsius; that's freezing, or 32° farenheit. Then go up or down nine degrees F for every five degrees C. Or even easier, just keep a few benchmarks in mind:

0° C = 32° F = *freezing*
5° C = 41° F = *cold*
10° C = 50° F = *chilly*
15° C = 59° F = *cool*
20° C = 68° F = *room temperature*
25° C = 77° F = *warm*
30° C = 86° F = *hot* (for England, at least)

Some radio stations give temperatures in fahrenheit and most newspapers use both scales.

Most Britons are much more comfortable around the metric system than Americans, but they still use inches, feet, and miles. You'll see many more references to metric measures in Britain, though, because of requirements of the European Union. Occasionally you'll still hear weights, especially a personal body weight, given in *stone*, as in "She weighs 9 stone 7." A *stone* is an old measure equal to 14 pounds, so 9 stone 7 would be 133 pounds. You might even still run across a bathroom scale graduated in stone and pounds.

Native Customs and Nasty Faux Pas

We said earlier that you're not likely to disgrace yourself and your country with an inadvertent slip, and we meant it. You can relax, because the English are used to tourists, not just from America but from all over Europe and the rest of the world. Frankly, Americans are among their favorites and they're willing to cut you a break as long as you're polite and at least *try* to abide by their customs.

That's not to say you won't make a little slip somewhere along the way. Societies are complex and we spend a lifetime learning our own culture. You won't pick up all the nuances of a new one in a week or two. So if you do something that gets you a dirty look and you're embarrassed, relax. Britain outlawed capital punishment years ago, so you're safe. Just learn from your mistake.

Here are a few basics of behavior that should get you through the first couple of days while you're learning the ropes. And here's a bit of advice, too: When in doubt, ask. Just say something like, "I've just come over on holiday from the United States, and I'm not sure what would be polite to do in this situation. Can you advise me?" People will respond well to a question like that, and chances are you'll find that you're expected to do just what you would at home!

The Ubiquitous Queue

The British line up (or "queue up") for everything. If there are only two people at a bus stop, they will form a neat line and board the bus single-file when it arrives. If there are 30 people waiting, they will never gather in a knot and shoulder their way on: their queue of 30 people will extend, single file, down the street. Cutting into line, or "jumping the queue," is *not* done and is extremely bad form. It's one of the few things you can do that's likely to earn you a reprimand from a stranger.

"Sorry."

London, you will notice right away, is a very crowded city. It's impossible to walk the streets and ride the tube without jostling someone occasionally. Don't say things like "Excuse me," or "I beg your pardon." The phrase is "Sorry" as you move along, or, if you've severely crushed somebody's toe, "Terribly sorry."

Words and Gestures

We're enchanted by their accents, they're amused by ours. Most of our words mean the same thing on both sides of the ocean, but the differences are unexpected, entertaining, and occasionally embarrassing. Appendix A provides a short glossary of words you might encounter that mean something different from what you might expect. Language differences might provide the basis for some of the best traveller's tales you bring home with you.

Have the members of your family listen especially for these kinds of things, and at lunch each day talk about the most interesting or perplexing language differences everyone has discovered:

- You'll be confused the first time you seek an office on the first floor of a building, only to find that it's one flight up from street level. (The street level is the "ground floor." The next flight up is the 1st floor—what we would call the 2nd floor—and so on.)

- You'll be embarrassed if you go into a shop to buy a pair of pants, and are shown to the underwear section. What you want are *trousers*.

- You'll be aghast if your landlady asks you if you'd like her to knock you up in the morning. She's merely offering to wake you with a polite tap at your door.

- You'll be amused by the names of some of the food items on many pub menus. But *spotted dick* is just a steamed pudding with raisins or currants usually served with hot custard sauce, *bangers and mash* is sausages with mashed potatoes, and *toad in the hole* is a sausage cooked in popover butter and baked.

Nonverbal language is not much different from that at home, but if you're gesturing to the innkeeper that you want two pints of beer, hold up two fingers with your palm toward him, like a "V for Victory" sign. Turning your hand the other way carries much the same meaning that ordering one pint by holding up your middle finger would in the United States.

English or British?

Most Americans think of these words as interchangeable, but they're not. You're usually safest with "British," which can be applied to anyone in England, Scotland, or Wales, although the latter two groups *might* prefer to be known as Scottish or Welsh. There's no sure way to win this battle; just do your best with the terminology and if somebody grumbles, well, you tried.

Meeting and Greeting People

One of the most pleasant parts of travelling is talking with people who live in the place you're visiting. You can see and learn about places you'll never find in the maps and guidebooks, and learn stories and local lore you'd never get from a tour guide. The British have a reputation for being uncommunicative, aloof, even cold. That's not altogether true, but they usually are not as open and ready to talk as Americans. If you're willing to go slowly, you'll find the British every bit as friendly and warm as anyone.

Perhaps because London is so crowded, people there cherish their privacy and can be slow to let outsiders in. We were once on a five-hour train ride to the southwest of England and were seated across a table from an English lady and her ten-year-old son. We made several gentle attempts to engage her in conversation, beginning with safe, neutral topics like the weather and the trains, but while we always received perfectly cheerful and polite replies, it was more than two hours before our companion began to talk a little more freely. By the time she and her son left the train, an hour before our own destination, we were chatting like neighbors. But the British, as a rule, prefer to take relationships more slowly than we do.

On the other hand, no one is more willing to help. We can't recall the number of times we've been standing on the sidewalk puzzling out our route somewhere, struggling over a map, when suddenly a Londoner has appeared beside us saying, "I beg your pardon, but may I help you find something?"

To live like a local means to experience the local culture, to talk to people and find out about your neighborhood. The British aren't keen on answering personal questions about their life and work, but they'll talk gladly about their house and garden, about their country, and about their travels. Shopkeepers, when they're not busy, and people who run B&Bs and small, family-operated hotels seem always to have a story at hand.

We fondly recall one tobacconist in Covent Garden who talked with pride of his service during World War II, particularly the day that King George VI came to inspect his regiment, stopped right in front of him, looked him in the eye, and nodding approval at his appearance, moved on.

Especially touching was the B&B lady in a tiny fishing village in Cornwall who explained why she and her neighbors fed the seagulls every afternoon. "There's not a family here that hasn't lost men in every generation to the sea," she told us. "My husband was lost at sea and one of my sons was, too. There's an old Cornish legend that seagulls are the souls of fishermen drowned at sea. We all take care of our gulls here in Cornwall; they might be our own men, come home to us again."

Meeting the Locals

While we've had many pleasant chats with people in the crowd waiting for the Changing of the Guard or standing in line to see the Crown Jewels, they are more likely to be tourists like us than local residents. There are some better places to meet the locals:

At street markets—Not the big ones like Petticoat Lane or Portobello Road, but smaller local markets. Try the one on Church Street near Regent's Park, or the market on Leather Lane in Holborn. Both are more likely to be populated by local residents.

At the park—The British make constant use of their parks. There are the big ones, of course, but a better place to meet the locals at rest is in the smaller parks and squares scattered throughout the city. We were enjoying the profusion of roses in Russell Square one evening when we were approached by an elderly man who sensed our interest. He'd been the gardener there for many years and he gave us in ten minutes a complete course in the care of roses. A week earlier we'd passed a pleasant hour in Thornbury Square in Islington talking with local people, watching their children playing soccer and practicing cricket.

At church—If your family goes to church at home, do so in London too. You'll probably find your denomination in London, but if you don't, there's sure to be a parish of the Anglican Church close by. The British are not great church-goers (studies put church membership at around fifteen percent) but you'll probably be noticed as a new face, welcomed warmly, and made to feel at home. Don't be concerned about doing the wrong thing at services. Being yourself and being sincere is what counts. You wouldn't criticize a stranger to your church at home for not knowing the local customs; the British won't either.

At the pub—We have already made much of the fact that a pub is more than just a bar, it's a local social center. At the local neighborhood pub you're less likely to find drunken patrons than at the bar down the street at home, but you will find area residents relaxing with friends, using their "local" as an extension of their living rooms.

Given the natural reserve of the English, what's the best way to break the ice in one of these settings? When you're spotted as a newcomer you might not have to—one of the locals might well approach you. But if not, ask somebody a question or seek advice. Identify yourself as an American tourist visiting London with your family, and ask someone what local places he thinks your kids might enjoy, or where your family can pass a special afternoon. The person you ask will be as pleasant and as willing to help as you would be if *he* were visiting in *your* home town.

Remember, though, that the idea of meeting the locals isn't like seeing the residents of the zoo or just soaking up local color. The idea is to learn more about the place you're visiting through contact with other people like yourself. Nothing will impress your children more with the idea that people are the same the world over than to meet and talk with ordinary people, people like themselves, from the places they visit. There's a natural tendency to look at London as a vast museum with the people there as merely additional exhibits. Meeting a few of them and spending a little time talking with them makes the point as nothing else can that British people, American people, *any* people are first of all—*people*. That's one of the most valuable reasons to take your family on a trip abroad.

Recommendations

↳ Pick up copies of two or three newspapers every day, not just to keep up with events but for insights into your host country.

↳ Make an effort to meet and talk with local residents, but don't press the effort too hard or too quickly; the English are less open and gregarious at first than Americans are.

↳ Try local products and ways of doing things, rather than what you're already familiar with.

For the latest updates to *London for Families*,
check our page on the World Wide Web at

http://www.as.udayton.edu/com/faculty/lain/lonfam.htm

Part II:
Seeing the Sights

I n Part I we talked about basic planning and survival skills. In Part II we'll show you the sights you came to see. We will pick through the thousands of attractions London holds to highlight the ones we believe have the broadest appeal to *families*. We'll also show you a smattering of more specialized things to see and do, just to hint at the scope of the possibilities in London, where there is truly something for everyone.

Unless you're planning to move to London, you won't have time to see nearly everything, but we'll tell you about the things you shouldn't miss and help you and your family sort through the myriad of other possibilities so you can line up days and nights filled with scenes that will create memories for everyone that will last forever. Those memories, after all, are the real reason for a trip like this!

9. Decisions, Decisions

A family holiday is different from one that's just for Mom and Dad. On the one hand, you'll probably do a greater variety of things because of the varied interests of the kids, going places they're excited about but which have much less interest for their parents (Rock Circus, anyone?). At the same time, Mom and Dad may have to forego some of the things they'd really like to do, like an elegant dinner cruise, or extra nights at the theatre.

This is more than made up for, though, by the wonderful family experience you're making together. This can be a very special vacation, creating bonds and memories that will last a lifetime—your family together in a foreign land.

Part II of *London for Families* will take you through a variety of attractions that might appeal to various members of your family. We'll give you a description of many places to consider—more than you can get to in one vacation—and tell you not only the things we like, but some of the things we think are overrated or not really suitable for a family.

We'd suggest that your whole family read these chapters to get a good feel for the possibilities that exist in London, and then, using the Planning Pages in Part III, let everybody list their top choices and vote for the things they would most like to see and do.

Decisions, Decisions

Everyone will have different priorities. The baseball fan might want to go to a cricket match, while the stuffed animal collector may think that a visit to Hamley's would be the highlight of any trip. Everybody should get their first choice, however. Even things that seem trivial to parents ("But you've already got *three* stuffed Paddingtons!") can fill a child's eyes with tears of excitement— even those of a normally sophisticated and aloof teenager.

Plan, But Don't Overdo It

It's important not to over-plan. Definitely make a list of the things you want to do, but don't create fixed timetables. Nothing spoils a vacation more than rushing madly through one attraction to get to the next one on time. You'll be pleasantly surprised by some of the places you go and want to spend more time there. Others will be less than you'd hoped for and can be cut short. There's a real tendency to reason that going so far and paying so much for a trip like this means that you have to squeeze as much as humanly possible into your days. But packing too much activity into too little time is just a recipe for short tempers and exhaustion. The itineraries in Chapter 19 give some examples of nicely-paced days.

Keep track of the most-favored attractions for each member of your family, rough them into your itinerary in ways that are most convenient, keeping in mind that some things may need to be changed depending on circumstances. A cricket match is a poor choice for a rainy day, for instance. It might be better to put that off until tomorrow and visit the Museum of the Moving Image today instead.

Secrets of Successful Sightseeing

You'll be seeing a wide variety of attractions, which can take many forms. You'll see museums, historic sites, churches, quaint streets, fascinating shops. To get the most out of them, a mix of contrasts is important.

London for Families

Try not to see two of the same kind of thing each day. Don't visit both the British Museum and the Natural History Museum on the same day; they'll run together in your mind and you'll forget which exhibits you saw where. Visiting both Westminster Abbey and St. Paul's Cathedral on the same day will reduce the impact and splendor of both. Mix it up. Spend 90 minutes in a museum, a half-hour in a park, 45 minutes in an interesting church, have lunch, take a slow walk by the Thames or down Whitehall, watch the buskers and do a little shopping in Covent Garden, and go back to the flat for supper.

One to two hours is long enough for most attractions. You couldn't see the entire British Museum in a year, so the difference between two hours and three won't dramatically alter your life. See the key exhibits and leave before you get tired. If there's time you can always come back another day. Children normally have shorter attention spans than adults, so staying in any one place too long will make them bored and restless.

That does *not* mean that you should flit wildly from attraction to attraction, though. Take things at a leisurely pace. Stop and relax every hour-and-a-half to two hours and do a little people watching. Get a snack and sit on a bench by the river, or feed the pigeons in Trafalgar Square. For a relaxing time mixed with sightseeing, consider a boat trip down the Thames, or a canal boat ride through Regent's Park. And no matter how busy you are, don't skip lunch or delay it too long. Tired or hungry people are crabby people.

Don't forget about the value of exercise. You'll probably be walking more in London than you do at home, but that won't be true every day. Some days you'll spend a lot of time standing while you see museums and other attractions, and standing on hard floors and pavement is much more tiring than walking. Kids usually have more energy than their parents, too, so what may be more-than-usual exercise for Mom and Dad might be less than many children are used to.

If that's the case, a romp in the park can be just the thing to stretch those cramped legs. Climbing to the top of St. Paul's or the Monument will not only burn off excess energy but provide spectacular birds-eye views of London. It's not easy to strike the perfect balance between too much activity and too little, but watch and listen to your kids and take your cues from them.

It's OK to Split Up Sometimes

If there are more favorite choices than available time, or if some attractions excite half your group and bore the other half, remember that you don't have to go everywhere in a pack. Split up. Once in planning a daytrip one member of our family really wanted to go to Stratford-upon-Avon, while another member said he was deeply interested in Canterbury. We had time for only one out-of-town trip, so Mom and two kids went to Stratford, Dad and one kid went to Canterbury, and everyone had a great day. We were back at our flat by suppertime with lots of sights and experiences to share. If we'd insisted on sticking together, at least one person would have had a disappointing day, and that reduces everybody's enjoyment.

The idea works on a smaller scale, too. Even mushing around in London in a pack isn't always necessary. It's fun to go somewhere together every day, but after lunch smaller groups might work better. You cover more ground, everyone sees more of what they want, and the kids are less likely to feel regimented and controlled.

Keep tabs on your younger ones

If some of the kids are old enough, and after everyone has had a few days to get the feel of the city, it's even all right—and this is hard the first time—to let them set out alone, or let a couple of older kids go together, without parents. Depending on the child, we'd say you could consider this for those at least fourteen. London is an extremely safe city (much more so than any large American city) and easy to get around in. The chance to be alone in London will give teens a memorable adventure, will give them self-confidence and self-esteem, as well as something to talk about with their friends when they get home. They are no more likely to get into trouble in London than they are at home, and they'll enjoy the trust and the freedom. The older a child is, the more he or she will probably enjoy a half day alone from time to time. It will do wonders for everyone's disposition and will provide good fodder for conversations later, too. Kids will be especially pleased when they stumble on something exciting that only they have seen, and which they can lead the whole family to later.

Every member of your family over the age of thirteen will probably feel comfortable on the tube after the first day or two, so no one is likely to get lost, but if they should, there's one quick fix. Taxis are plentiful, and can whisk a confused tourist back to his or her lodgings in a flash, almost always for less than £10 and probably for less than half that. Everyone, even adults, should carry a city map, a tube map, taxi fare, and identification with London address whenever they're out and about.

Plan Free Time

Besides the occasional stops to catch your breath on sightseeing excursions, plan a half day of free time every few days. A picnic in the park is a lovely way to spend a sunny afternoon. Find a spot in Hyde Park near the Serpentine, or in Regent's Park with a view of the Rose Garden, or a favorite spot of your own, and just take food and drinks and something to read, spread out on the grass, and relax. Picnic items are inexpensive and a few hours in the park gives everyone the chance to talk, and to be as active or as quiet as

It's always fun to watch the buskers

he or she chooses. There's probably a square or park within a block or two of your lodgings and that's a great place to spend an hour after dinner, too.

Evenings are good times for going to the theatre or to watch people in Covent Garden or Trafalgar Square, or for long walks along the river or canal. But also spend some evenings in your hotel or flat, just relaxing and watching TV, or playing a game. Everyone will find the television shows interesting for a while at least, and evenings offer a good chance for each person to tell about their favorite sights and experiences of the day, as well as to make plans for the next day.

Pace can be the critical ingredient of a successful family vacation. Too hectic a schedule will make everyone irritable, but free time and relaxing activities carefully placed as part of every itinerary will add to everyone's enjoyment of the trip.

Recommendations

✔ Talk ahead of time about what everyone wants to see, and make sure everyone gets his or her first choice.

✔ Mix up your activities each day. Variety provides spice.

- Don't spend more than two hours on anything unless everyone wants more time.

- Plan free time.

- Let teens venture into the city on their own occasionally, if they wish.

10. Museums

There are at least 60 important museums in London and scores of smaller ones—and that's not even considering art galleries! There's no way you can hope to see them all unless you move to London and dedicate yourself to the task with some sort of pathological singlemindedness. Besides, many of them are extremely specialized and would send you off to the nearest pub before you'd finished the first exhibit.

We won't try to review all of London's museums in this chapter; we won't even try to list them all. We'll focus on the museums we think will appeal broadly to most families, and we'll give you some sense of the scope of the London museum scene. Your family will make its choices based on the things its members think are most appealing.

We admit a bias toward the kids in the family here. Maybe you *do* have a child who is excited about plants and flowers, but in most families, the **Museum of Garden History** (*Lambeth Palace Road, SE1*), for example, will appeal mostly to Mom and Dad. We're looking for family fare, and even though Captain Bligh of Mutiny on the Bounty fame is buried here and lovely flowers abound, most kids will spend a maximum of twelve minutes here before pointing out the fact that they're hungry, thirsty, and tired. So let's start with two can't-miss places:

The British Museum and British Library (*Great Russell Street, WC1: free admission. Tube: Tottenham Court Road—Central and Northern lines*).

There may be two or three other museums in the world that have the credentials to dispute the claim, but the British Museum is arguably the greatest single museum on earth. You could spend your entire vacation here and not begin to digest its wonders. How then to stick to our rule giving us a maximum of two hours in any attraction? Cherry-pick shamelessly!

Talk about what you want to see. The British Museum has the greatest collections in the world of Egyptian, Greek, and Roman antiquities outside their native lands. The *Michelin Guide to London* and a handful of other books give a detailed, room-by-room guide to the contents of the museum. But we recommend starting with the Egyptology collection.

Go in the main entrance and start on the ground floor (in America we'd call it the first floor). Turn to the left, through the shop, then right into the Egyptian Sculpture Gallery and let your jaw drop in wonder! Here you'll see sights straight out of the history books: the statue of Ramses II, who pursued Moses to the Red Sea, the great Lions of Amenophis; the Rosetta Stone, which unlocked the secrets of the hieroglyphics. Wander among the colossal sculptures plundered from Egypt and marvel at their power.

But don't marvel too long. It's tempting to spend your two hours right here, but more wonders await. At the end of the gallery, take the stairs to the upper floor. Now you will find yourself in the Upper Egyptian Galleries, featuring room after room of ancient Egyptian wall paintings, artifacts, and best of all, scores of mummies, some nearly 3,000 years old, preserved nearly intact!

It's worth an extra fifteen minutes to go back down the staircase you came up and make your way through some of the Greek artifacts in the rooms beyond the Egyptian Sculpture Gallery, heading for the Duveen Gallery along the west side of the building. This room holds the famous Elgin Marbles, the magnificent sculptures that once faced the Parthenon at Athens. But there's more to see.

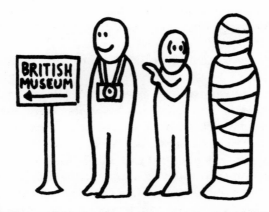

You'll see all kinds of neat things at the British Museum

Return to the entrance, but this time turn to the right. Now you're entering the British Library. You'll pass through the bookstore and discover in the galleries beyond a treasure trove of marvels to delight anyone who ever got a grade higher than a D– in history or literature class.

On display in these rooms are original signed letters by most of the monarchs and prime ministers of England. Gaze on a letter of Henry VIII to Cardinal Wolsey or on the signature of Queen Elizabeth I on the death warrant of her former lover, the Earl of Essex. See the Magna Carta, the first stirrings of a freedom that would be fully realized in America's Declaration of Independence more than 550 years later.

Original manuscripts by the literary and cultural greats of the world pack the room. Your children will see Lewis Carroll's handwritten *Alice in Wonderland*, with illustrations drawn by the author himself. Here, too, are poems by Wordsworth, musical scores by Mozart and Beethoven, and items like Robert Scott's diary, written as he sat freezing to death after reaching the South Pole. The first printed copy of Shakespeare's works, along with documents signed personally by him, occupy places of honor. This list barely hints at the scope of the collection.

When you've seen all this, you've barely scratched the surface of the British Museum. Unless you plan to spend your entire holiday here, however, there are countless other places clamoring for your attention. So save some of the other exhibits for a rainy day.

Museum of the Moving Image (*South Bank, SE: admission charge but family rate available. Tube: Waterloo—Northern and Bakerloo lines*).

Does anyone in your family like television or movies? Then a real treat awaits. MOMI (pronounced *moe*-mee), as everyone here calls it, is a wonderful, fun museum experience for everyone. It offers lots of hands-on opportunities as well as interesting, if more traditional, displays. Exhibits are arranged chronologically and cover every type of—well—moving image imaginable, beginning with hand shadows cast by firelight on cave walls and leading up to satellite TV and computer animation.

Kids will be fascinated at how early drawings and photographs were made to appear to move with the simplest technology; they'll laugh at the idea of people feeding coins into Nickelodeons to watch movies, and at the impossibly clunky tiny-screened television sets of the 1930s.

While their parents are admiring Fred Astaire's evening clothes, they may be looking at Charlie Chaplin's "Little Tramp" costume, at some of the original Muppets, or at Dr. Who's TARDIS.

Everyone can rest their feet a while in the movie theatre watching a vintage film, then move on to learn about newsreels, special effects, cartoons, and

---

Getting Involved at MOMI

The Museum of the Moving Image is packed with opportunities for involvement. Most galleries have costumed interpreters who will answer your questions and who, at intervals, become part of the show themselves, but who always stay in character. (Ask someone running an 1880s magic lantern show what he thinks of television, for instance, and you'll be met with a blank expression and a puzzled "Telly-vision? What's that?")

much more. But the things you can *see* are only half the fun. There's so much to *do* as well. The sidebar on this page describes some of many hands-on experiences and activities MOMI has to offer.

MOMI is another museum where it can be hard to invoke our two-hour rule. But London beckons, and two hours will tire even the kids. It's time to move on.

Museums for Every Interest

In the rest of this chapter we'll break down some of the remaining museums into broad categories. If someone in your family is interested in the subject generally, these will provide exciting possibilities for exploration. The ones we list here have been selected for their appeal

The interpreters try to get visitors involved in what's happening, and while no one is ever pressured to play along, it's all part of the fun. One of the authors was snagged by a "1920s Hollywood casting director" and taught to do the Charleston for his big "screen test." On another trip, the same person was recruited to lead a turn-of-the-century sing-along of "A Bicycle Built for Two." (Warning: Never go to MOMI with Larry. He's sure to embarrass you.) Another member of our group starred in a 1930s Western, swaggering out of the saloon and gunning down another tourist on the streets of Dodge in front of authentic lights, cameras, and a score of other laughing tourists. Younger children are invited into the action, too.

Besides that, they can draw their own cartoons and make their own animations. There's one exhibit where they can see how Superman flies. Everyone who wants to can become part of the exhibit and see themselves on television, flying above the River Thames toward Tower Bridge. Elsewhere, the future Dan Rather or Barbara Walters in your family can read the evening news from a teleprompter in front of TV cameras, then watch the tape of their performance.

No wonder MOMI has, in its less than ten-year history, won a barrelful of awards and has become recognized as the world's leading museum of television and film.

across rather wide ranges of age and interest. But do all the reading you can in planning your trip: there are countless things to see in London and a child's interest too narrow for us to include here may turn out to be the perfect stop on your trip.

Toys

The **Bethnal Green Museum of Childhood** (*Cambridge Heath Road, E2: free admission. Tube: Bethnal Green—Central line*) is run by the Victoria & Albert Museum and holds the national collection of toys and models, one of the largest such collections in the world. You'll discover a wide array here, including trains, doll houses, games, toy soldiers, puppets, and much more. If the kids haven't started their Christmas lists yet, this, the best of London's toy museums, will give them more ideas than you can afford. Note that you can't actually *play* with the toys. Mostly, they're enclosed in glass cases.

The **London Toy and Model Museum** (*23 Craven Hill, W2: admission charge. Tube: Queensway or Lancaster Gate—Central line; Bayswater—Circle and District lines*) specializes in trains and models of all sorts, with nice collections of doll houses, teddy bears, and toy animals, soldiers, and cars. This museum has gone through a lengthy remodelling recently, which has made it much livelier and more modern.

Pollock's Toy Museum (*1 Scala Street, W1: admission charge. Tube: Goodge Street—Northern line*) is more than a hundred years old and has a fine collection of children's playthings of the past, with an emphasis on dolls and toy animals; its modern items are much more limited. Children may enjoy the other two museums more than this one, which has more of a dusty Victorian feel to it. Both Charles Dickens and Robert Louis Stevenson knew Pollock's, and the place still evokes their feel.

Science and Nature

There are so many choices it's hard to narrow them down to a handful. But rich as they are, places like the **Freud Museum** or the

The Museum of Childhood is a wonderful place to see dollhouses and miniatures

Museum of Mankind have an appeal that is perhaps less broad than some others. Here are some good choices. The first two are among London's most popular family attractions, always crowded with tourists and school groups, but worth as much time as you care to give them.

The **Natural History Museum** (*Cromwell Road, SW7: admission charge but family ticket available. Tube: South Kensington—Piccadilly, District, and Circle lines*) is part of a complex of great museums (including the Science Museum and the Victoria & Albert Museum), and has what you'd expect in this sort of museum. There are dinosaur skeletons, fossils, and artifacts of early humans, with vast collections of animal specimens and a large exhibit on man's place in evolution. The Geological Museum, with its stunning collection of gemstones, is now a part of the Natural History Museum. New exhibits give dramatic views of volcanoes and allow you to feel what it's like to be in an earthquake.

At the **Science Museum** *(located on Exhibition Road behind the Natural History Museum with a similar admission price and policy)*, everything related to science and technology is here: space flight, airplanes,

Tip: The Science Museum and the Natural History Museum are open until 6 p.m. in the summer, but they stop charging admission at 4:30 or 5 o'clock, depending on the day. Crowds also begin to thin out as the dinner hour approaches, so these might be a good bet for your last stop of the afternoon.

trains, autos, communication, energy in all its forms, and a special children's gallery. The museum is packed full of hands-on displays that will fascinate everyone from the youngest child to the adults. The galleries depicting the history of medicine are intriguing for everyone, and more than a little hair-raising.

The **London Zoo** almost closed a few years ago because of financial problems, but it is now on firm footing and is a fun place to spend a sunny morning or afternoon. *(Regent's Park, NW1: admission charge but family ticket available. Tube: All are about a 15-minute walk from the zoo. Ride a double-decker bus. No. 274 from Marble Arch or Baker Street will take you there quickly.)* In addition to the usual zoo animals, kids love to see the pandas, and a brand-new Children's Zoo has been added.

Soldiers and Sailors

London was once the seat of the largest empire the world has ever seen, so it's natural that the city abounds in military associations. Besides spectacles like the Changing of the Guard and Trooping the Color (see Chapter 11), and memorials like the Cenotaph (in

Museums

The Zoo is fun for all ages

Whitehall) and the Grave of the Unknown Warrior (in Westminster Abbey), there are many interesting museums for the military-minded.

The **Imperial War Museum** (*Lambeth Road, SE1: admission charge but family ticket available. Free after 4:30. Tube: Lambeth North— Bakerloo line*) focuses on the effects of war. First-time visitors are often concerned that the museum glorifies war and arms, but the effect is quite the reverse, taking neither a pro- nor anti-military stand but showing how war touches the lives of both soldiers and civilians. This museum, started during World War I, stands on the site of the early 19th-century Bethlem Royal Hospital, called "Bedlam," a lunatic asylum.

A branch of the Imperial War Museum is the **Cabinet War Rooms** (*King Charles Street, SW1, near Parliament: admission charge. Tube: Westminster—Circle and District lines*). This was Winston Churchill's London bunker during the Blitz, a series of nineteen underground rooms from which the British Government operated during the dark nights of World War II. There are meeting rooms, the map room with its furnishings intact, the communication room, from which Churchill kept in touch with Roosevelt and Stalin, even Churchill's bedroom, from which he made many of his inspirational speeches to the nation. The rooms were sealed after the war and left just as they were at the time. Now they provide an interesting glimpse into more recent history.

Anchored in the River Thames is the **H.M.S.** *Belfast (Tooley Street, SE1 on the south side of the Thames: admission charge. Tube: London Bridge—Northern line)*, a World War II cruiser, the largest the Royal Navy ever built. Most of the ship is open to visitors and there are several special exhibits, such as one on D-Day and another on the evolution of the battleship.

Literature

Here, too, London offers far too many wonderful choices to make life easy. Almost every important English-speaking writer passed through London and many lived and worked here. Your children often study the same writers in school that you did so they've got the background to enjoy places like the ones we suggest here—and maybe picking up some grade-building pictures and souvenirs to take back to school.

The **Globe Theatre** *(Bankside, SE1: admission charge. Tube: London Bridge—Northern line; or Cannon Street—Circle line)* isn't the Bard's original, of course. That burned down in 1613. But American film producer Sam Wanamaker built this authentic reproduction just a block or two from the original site on Park Street (although, sadly, he died shortly before the project was completed). Every high school student studies Shakespeare, and this is a unique opportunity to see his plays performed exactly as they were 400 years ago—same location, a theatre indistinguishable from the original (except for fireproofing and public toilets!), same afternoon and evening performances with standing room for the "groundlings" in front of the stage. What an experience to take back to English Lit class! The **Shakespeare Globe Museum** is nearby in Bear Gardens Alley. We'll give you more information about the entire area in the next chapter.

Dickens House *(48 Doughty Street, WC1: admission charge. Tube: Russell Square—Piccadilly line)* is the only one of Dickens' numerous London homes still standing. He wrote several of his many novels and stories here, including *Oliver Twist*, and the home is filled with authentic furnishings. An interesting one-man show recreating a Dickens lecture is often performed here one evening each week. Most other sites closely connected with Dickens have disappeared.

Sherlock Holmes Museum (*239 Baker Street, NW1, renumbered as 221B: admission charge. Tube: Baker Street—Bakerloo, Jubilee, Circle, and Metropolitan lines*). Sherlock Holmes, along with King Arthur and Robin Hood, is one of the most famous Englishmen who never lived. And he still gets thousands of letters a year, addressed to his flat at 221B Baker Street, near Regent's Park.

Unfortunately there is no such address as 221B Baker Street, so the letters are delivered to the nearest building, a branch of the Abbey National Bank, which employs a secretary just to answer Holmes' mail. A bit further up the street there *is* a building which calls its address 221B, set up as a Sherlock Holmes Museum.

Holmes fans will find this extremely well done. You'll be greeted by a "policeman" in a uniform of the 1880s and shown up the stairs to Holmes' sitting room, and your credentials as a Sherlockian may be tested when you're presented with two chairs and invited to sit in the detective's usual place. (Choose the one with its back to the window; Holmes, of course, always wanted the light to fall upon the face of his client sitting opposite him.) This museum is probably not worth the more than £5 admission for anyone who hasn't read some of the Holmes mysteries.

Two Other Major Names

These are considered two of London's major museums, but there may be less here to appeal to the whole family than at some other places.

If you liked rummaging about in your Great Aunt Agatha's attic, you'll feel right at home in the **Victoria & Albert Museum** (*Cromwell Road, SW7: admission free but donation requested. Tube: South Kensington—Piccadilly, Circle, and District lines*). It includes a little bit of everything, but some might enjoy the fine collections of clothes from 1600 to the present and the fabulous jewelry exhibit. There's a fine collection of armor, though it won't match what you saw at the Tower. Overall this is probably a better museum for adults than for children.

The **Museum of London** (*150 London Wall, EC2: admission charge but free after 4:30 (closed Mondays). Tube: St. Paul's—Central line; or Barbican—Circle and Metropolitan lines*) tells the story of the place you're visiting, but perhaps in more detail than some family members really want. But it has nice Roman and Celtic artifacts, a good exhibit on the fire of 1666 that destroyed the city, and a Punch and Judy display. Everyone enjoys gawking at the elaborately gilded Lord Mayor's Coach, and there are rooms set up to reflect domestic life during various periods of history in London. The younger the children, the more you'll need to be selective in this museum: there's much of interest, but also much that smaller children might find tedious. The gift shop here is excellent, packed with unique souvenirs of the city.

A Potpourri of Other Museums

A number of other places, less easily categorized, are either worth a visit or are museums you'll hear about and should consider if you have the time and interest. For some family members one of these could be the highlight of the trip while leaving everyone else bored to tears.

Opinions vary widely about London's famous waxworks museum, **Madam Tussaud's** (*Marylebone Road, NW1: admission charge. Tube: Baker Street—Bakerloo, Jubilee, Circle, and Metropolitan lines*). Half the people who go there think it's the best thing in London, while the other half feel they've wasted their time and money. The wax figures are sometimes very lifelike and sometimes hokey, but it's one way to see scores of famous leaders and celebrities up close and (almost) personal. A combined ticket to the wax museum and to the Planetarium next door is available at a discount.

More wax figures are available at the **London Dungeon** (*28–34 Tooley Street, SE1: admission charge. Tube: London Bridge—Northern line*) but these are much more gruesome and small children are *not* encouraged to go. But fans of horror movies will enjoy (if that's the word for it) the place. Be prepared for torture, plague, fire, and the headsman's axe.

There are more oddities to be found at the **Guinness World of Records** (*The Trocadero, Piccadilly Circus, W1: admission charge but family ticket available. Tube: Piccadilly Circus—Piccadilly and Bakerloo lines*). There are special effects and multimedia displays galore, and if some of them are overdone and corny, at least there's lots to see. Trivia buffs will glory in it.

London has the best-known city transport system in the world and the **London Transport Museum** (*Covent Garden, WC1: admission charge but family ticket available. Tube: Covent Garden—Piccadilly line*) commemorates every red double-decker, tube train, and black taxi. It's modern and fun, but the gift shop may be better, with some of the best souvenir shopping in town.

So there are 20 museums. Is that enough to keep your family busy? If not, there are medical museums (Florence Nightingale Museum, Old Operating Theatre Museum, Museum of the History of Medicine) or religious museums (Jewish Museum, Museum of Methodism), or sports and leisure museums (Cricket Museum, Postal Museum, Musical Museum, Coffee and Tea Museum, Windmill Museum), and dozens of others. We don't know *exactly* what the members of your family find exciting, but whatever it is, there's almost certainly a museum dedicated to it in London!

Recommendations

✔ The Museum of the Moving Image is a top family attraction with a variety of well-presented exhibits.

✔ Look for tie-ins with your children's school subjects like history and literature. Seeing first-hand the things they talk about in school will help them do better and will raise their self-esteem.

✔ The hands-on exhibits at the Science Museum are the best in London.

11. History and Pageantry

A nyone who loves history, royalty, or pageantry will find London to be absolutely breathtaking. This is the city of Henry VIII and his assorted wives, the city of William Shakespeare and Sherlock Holmes, a city that was nearly wiped out by a plague one year and burned to the ground the next. London was a city that during two world wars was attacked from the air by dirigibles, airplanes, and rockets, but whose defiance inspired its armies and allies as nothing else could. Monarchs have ruled from London for more than 1,200 years, and the largest empire the world has yet known had its seat here. London oozes history from every pore.

Londoners are also aware of their own history, probably much more than we Americans are of our own. London is a city of stories. A pub keeper in Bloomsbury will explain why the windows in the hotel across from his pub have been bricked up for two centuries. The fellow sitting next to you at the cricket match will know more about the policies of the government of King Henry II in 1165 than your next-door neighbor will know of the policies of the government of Lyndon Johnson in 1965. Your taxi driver will explain how driving on the left makes more sense when you know that it got started in the Middle Ages.

History and Pageantry

In this chapter we'll hit some of the historical high spots that might interest some members of your family, and maybe tell a few stories along the way.

The Tower of London

There's no better place to start than the **Tower of London**. The Tower has been a royal palace, a prison, a military fortress, a zoo, a mint, an observatory, and a warehouse for old records, among other things. It is still an active military fort and troops are quartered here.

The Tower of London isn't just a tower; it's really a castle with a moat, stone walls, and a great iron gate, and many buildings inside, including a massive four-story building called the White Tower in the center. The White Tower was built more than 900 years ago by William the Conqueror after he invaded the country. William wasn't universally popular and he felt he needed a stronghold if he was going to hold the land he conquered. The Tower must have been an impressive and intimidating sight sitting atop a hill, whitewashed and gleaming in the sun, looking down on London.

Subsequent monarchs enlarged and strengthened the castle. Towers and turrets were added in the 1200s and a number of other buildings constructed inside the walls. A set of walls still further out was added before 1400, and while restoration and construction have continued, the Tower looks today very similar to the way it would have looked 600 years ago, although the moat, which had become a stinking and unhealthy cesspool, was drained in the last century.

The Tower is relatively pricey to get into, more than £8 for adults, but a family ticket is available for about £22 and there are discounts for students and senior citizens. There are few things in London more worth the money, however, and even though we've said not to spent more than 90 minutes or so in any museum, you'll want to spend a half day there. It's not just a single museum—it's a whole complex of exhibits and experiences. Here are the highlights:

1. The Crown Jewels—
This is one of England's most popular and crowded attractions and waits of more than an hour on summer afternoons used to be common.

> ***Tip:*** *Get to the Tower when it opens at 9:30 (2 o'clock on Sunday) and go straight to the Jewel House. The lines get longer and slower later in the day but there's no competition first thing in the morning.*

But the Jewel House has been revamped recently and the line moves more swiftly now, and it's easier to see the fabulous crowns and other regalia. The new Jewel House takes you through the exhibits in a way that allows you to linger over the ones you like best, and huge video screens give you glimpses of the goodies and fascinating narratives of their histories as you make your way through the line.

The crowns and ceremonial robes of the monarchs are on display here, and so is a vast array of gold table service, state trumpets, swords, scepters, and all the royal trappings you can imagine. The pieces are historic. One crown is made from an older one which may date back before William the Conqueror, and contains a ruby known to have been worn by Henry V in 1415. The Royal Sceptre contains the Star of Africa diamond, the largest in the world. The exhibit will leave you drooling.

*2. Take a Tour—*After going through the Jewel House, return to the path inside the entrance (the Middle Tower) and join a tour given by one of the Yeoman Warders. The tours are free, and will give you an orientation to the place, as well as much interesting history and lore. The tours are entertaining and last about 45 minutes. You'll miss much of the significance of the Tower if you skip the tour. It's worth your time.

The Yeoman Warders, sometimes incorrectly called the Beefeaters (the similarly-dressed guards at St. James's Palace), are interesting in themselves. All are former noncommissioned officers in the British military who have at least 21 years of spotless service. They actually live in the Tower with their families and will usually be

Visitors are seldom beheaded at the Tower nowadays

glad to chat about life inside the fortress, including the history of their own apartment and the ghosts they've seen. Look over the East Wall of the Tower on the Wall Walk and you'll see their homes, a playground for their children, and the tennis court for the use of their families—which does look just a bit out of place in these otherwise ancient surroundings. If you visit the Tower on certain state holidays, the guards will be wearing their scarlet Tudor dress uniforms, a sight that just begs for a photograph. Most days they wear their less ornate blue "undress" uniforms.

The tour will take you past some of the most historic buildings, which you can go inside on your own later, and tell you about what has happened in each over the centuries, like the Bell Tower where the future Queen Elizabeth I was held prisoner by her sister "Bloody" Mary, or the Bloody Tower, where Sir Walter Raleigh was held prisoner for many years before his execution. You'll see Traitor's Gate, where prisoners arrived by boat, and you'll hear about the ravens who live in the Tower and whose continuing presence there, legend has it, ensures that the monarchy will never fall.

The tour continues past the site of the block on Tower Green where Henry VIII ended his marriage to Anne Boleyn by having her head cut off, and finishes in the chapel of St. Peter ad Vincula (St.

Peter in Chains), the Tower church, in which are buried three queens of England and hundreds of other nobles.

At the end of the tour a tip of about 50p to the Warder is appreciated but is never required.

3. *Take a Wall Walk*—Near the steps inside the inner wall opposite Traitor's Gate is the entrance to the Wall Walk. Climb the steps to the top of the inner wall to the broad walkway along its top. This is a wonderful walk that takes about a half-hour. When you come out on the wall you're facing the River Thames and have an exciting view of Tower Bridge on one side, and a comprehensive view of the interior of the Tower on the other side. As you walk along the wall you'll pass through several other towers with exhibits explaining their histories and development, often with costumed interpreters. Best is the exhibit in the Wakefield Tower, showing how it would have looked when King Henry VI lived here in the 1470s. Look down on the fragment of the 2,000 year-old Roman wall still standing in the courtyard.

The Salt Tower at the southwest corner is sometimes closed to the public. If it is, you can rejoin the wall walk just past the Salt Tower. The walk ends at the Martin Tower, which once housed the Crown Jewels. In simpler times the guard here would have

> **Tip:** *For travellers who want more historical background, we recommend reading* A Traveller's History of England *or* A Traveller's History of London. *Both books are delightful and make ideal before-you-go reading. The one on London condenses 2000 years of history into a lively, readable format which will prove particularly inviting for history buffs who want to have the book in hand while visiting parks, museums, and historical sites around London.*

let you try on the crown of state for a bribe of one penny.

When you come down from the Martin Tower you'll likely encounter the long line into the torture chamber exhibit in the Bowyer Tower. It's free, so if you're curious, go ahead; it will take no more than ten minutes to look at the exhibition. If the kids are *really* interested in torture, however, there are more grisly choices.

History and Pageantry

One is the London Dungeon, a fifteen-minute walk away on the other side of the river on Tooley Street near London Bridge Station (see Chapter 10). It's expensive, though, and admission costs about as much as that to the Tower itself. Young children might well find it too gruesome.

4. Enter the Beauchamp Tower—This tower (pronounced *Beech-um*) is near St. Peter Chapel and is worth a fifteen-minute visit. Like many other buildings in the Tower, it has served as a prison, but here the walls are covered with the graffiti prisoners have carved into the walls. Many inscriptions are more than 400 years old. There is usually a Yeoman Warder in this tower to point out the work of interesting prisoners and to answer questions.

5. The White Tower—At the center of the complex is the keep of William the Conqueror. It was begun in 1078 and has walls 100 feet high and ten feet thick. It has served as a royal residence for a score of monarchs, and is now a museum that is worth an hour of your time. Hundreds of old weapons fill its rooms, along with suits of armor and cannons. While further restoration work is in progress through 1998, some parts of the White Tower are closed to visitors. But don't miss the Chapel of St. John on the second floor, a beautiful and peaceful oasis of quiet. In this chapel men kept vigil all night before being knighted in the morning, and the monarch kept vigil the night before being crowned. It is a superb example of Norman architecture. Even during restoration, Yeoman Warders escort visitors to this special place.

There are countless other sights to see in the Tower, other buildings and museums. The Lains haven't yet gotten their fill of it. But take some time to find a spot on a bench and watch the people and rest your feet. There's a snack bar in the southeast corner of the grounds, outside the wall, which is a good place to stop for an ice cream bar on a hot day. There's a large gift shop along the South Wall if you're so inclined.

There is one more site at the Tower that's worth an hour of your time, but you'll have to return later to see it, after the Tower is closed for the day.

6. *The Ceremony of the Keys*—Each night the Tower is locked in a ceremony that has been going on without a miss for more than 700 years. Visitors with passes are admitted to the Tower grounds at about 9:30 p.m. through the main gate and escorted to the viewing area near Traitor's Gate. A Yeoman Warder explains what is to take place and that photography and taping are forbidden. The ceremony begins at 9:40 and lasts precisely 20 minutes as the gates are locked one by one and the keys to the Tower are escorted to safekeeping by armed guards. The ceremony ends with a bugler playing *The Last Post*, the British equivalent of *Taps*. Once the Tower is locked for the night and visitors escorted out, no one is supposed to be permitted to enter or leave. The Tower even has its own resident physician in case anyone is taken ill during the night.

The ceremony is impressive in its solemnity and in the fact that it has been going on in all sorts of weather, during bombings and revolutions, for seven centuries. In the summer, however, there may be as many as 50 or 60 visitors watching the ceremony, which is distracting. We've never attended during a sleet storm in February but that would probably give a more lonely, eerie feel to the proceedings.

Passes are free but must be requested in writing in advance. Write to:

> The Resident Governor
> HM Tower of London
> London EC2 U.K.

and request a pass. State your preferred date, along with two or three alternate dates, and how many will be in your party.

Make your request several weeks early and, if you're writing from the United States, enclose a self-addressed envelope and an International Reply Coupon for about a dollar, available from any post office. (Don't stamp the envelope: U.S. stamps are no good mailed from another country. That's what the IRP is for.)

Buckingham Palace

Until recently the closest tourists could get to the inside of Buckingham Palace was to visit the gift shop and art gallery in the Royal Mews—in the grounds, to be sure, but hardly a chance of bumping into Her Majesty. Seems right: confine the tourists to the place where they used to keep the horses. Since 1993, however, tourists have been permitted to view several rooms in the Palace while the royals are vacationing during August and September. It's one of the costliest tourist attractions in an already expensive town, and reviews have been decidedly mixed.

Frankly, you can see other grand residences just as ornate and even more historic for less than half the money. If the idea of tramping about in the home of the reigning queen appeals to you and you don't mind shelling out upwards of £50 for a family of four to gawk at the Windsors' dining room, go for it! But wait until near the end of your trip. By then you may be weary of stately mansions and will be glad you spent the money going to the theatre.

There's a marvelous free show at the Palace every day, however, and we recommend that you try it once: the famous Changing of the Guard.

Actually the guard changes many times each day. Those poor guards would get pretty tired of standing under the hot sun in their wool tunics and tall bearskin hats for an entire day! But at 11:30 each morning is the big ceremonial change.

It's best to arrive by 11 o'clock because the crowd gets pretty thick. There are two good places to watch the action: take your pick. Our favorite is from in front of the Victoria Monument directly in front of the palace gates. Here you can see the regiments marching smartly into and out of the palace grounds and get a good view of the band concert that comes during the middle of the ceremony. It's a fine spot to be stationed with a camera or camcorder to see the troops filing past. But you can't see much of what's going on inside the fence.

Many people prefer to stand right in front of the fence. It's not such a good location to see the guards on parade, but easier to see

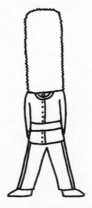

Some guards need changing at once!

the marching about they do inside the grounds as they change stations.

One of the best parts of the ceremony is the chance to talk to all the other people around while you're waiting for it to begin, or while you're killing time during some of the slow moving action. We've talked to people from all over the world there— even Londoners!

The Change is definitely worth going to once. You'll never forget the precision marching, the colorful uniforms, the gleaming bayonets, the stir-

Changing Some Other Guards

There are other changes of guard you might want to see instead, or to compare: The guard changes at the Tower each day at the same time as at Buckingham Palace. While it's smaller and without the band, the ceremony is still impressive.

Another guard change, this one on horseback, takes place each day at 11 a.m. (10 a.m. on Sunday) at the Horse Guards along Whitehall, about halfway between Trafalgar Square and Parliament. The Horse Guards also go through an inspection ceremony each day at 4 p.m. At other times, horses and riders are on guard outside the building and visitors often stand beside them for memorable photographs.

ring music. But you never know what the choice of music might be. First time Larry went to the ceremony he was expecting the band to play things like *God Save the Queen* and *Rule Britannia*. His most lasting memory of that ceremony, though, is of the band disappearing down the street at the end, loudly playing *New York, New York*.

If you happen to be passing by the Palace when they're changing the guard at other times, there's no pomp and ceremony, but the movements are performed, even in the middle of the night, with the same precision and military snap as you'll see at noon.

Changing the Horse Guards

Shakespeare Country

Everyone in the family who's finished at least a year of high school has read some Shakespeare. No writer has influenced our language and literature more than he, and it's exciting to see some of the many places connected with his life. If there's an English Lit class in the future of somebody in the family, be sure to shoot photos, slides, or videos of these sites: They *will* help with the grade in the class!

The best place to experience Shakespeare is south of the River Thames, in the part of London called Southwark (pronounced *Suth*-ik). Spend a couple of hours walking around this area for some great views of the river and for the feel of stepping back a little into history.

Four hundred years ago, in Shakespeare's day, this was the seedy part of town. It's still a little grimier than the more touristy areas north of the Thames, but it's just as safe and just as historic. But the things associated with it more than four centuries ago were decidedly disreputable. That's why Shakespeare hung out down here. He wasn't, so far as we know, a particularly dirty old man, but he *was* an actor, and the theatre wasn't a respectable profession. In fact, playhouses were banned from the City north of the river and had to be located here, on the south side.

There were even shadier activities than theatre-going down here. The brothels and prostitutes conducted business in Southwark, and there was much drinking and plenty of gambling at the local cock-fighting and bear-baiting arenas in the neighborhood. The area is no longer a dive, but we'll see some evidence of Southwark's unsavory past.

But let's begin by going to church. Start at the south end of London Bridge. (That's the next bridge upstream from the ornate Tower Bridge.) Less than a block from the river you'll come to *Southwark Cathedral*. You can easily weary of touring important churches in Europe, but this one is worth spending a few minutes visiting. Aside from being old (mostly 1300s and 1400s) it has some interesting associations, especially with William Shakespeare.

To begin with, the Bard knew this church well. His playhouse was just up the street and he almost certainly attended church services in this very building. There is an interesting memorial to Shakespeare in this church, consisting of an alabaster statue and a stained-glass window with scenes from many of his plays. Ask your family literary expert how many he or she can figure out.

History and Pageantry

As you walk through the sanctuary behind the altar, look at the inscriptions on the stones beneath your feet. They mark the graves of some of the many men and women who are buried in the church. Eventually you'll find the stone of Edmund Shakespeare. That's Will's younger brother, an actor in his company, who died in 1607 and is buried here.

There's one other item most Americans find interesting: the Harvard Chapel, dedicated to John Harvard, who was born nearby, but who emigrated for the colonies in 1638 and founded a college you may have heard of.

Outside the cathedral is a quiet courtyard, a favorite spot for lunchtime brown-baggers and tourists with tired feet. When you've rested, leave by the rear, or west, end of the courtyard. You'll see Borough Market, one of London's chief fruit and vegetable markets. Now turn right, behind the church, and head back toward the river. You'll come upon an old trading vessel, the *Kathleen and May*, now drydocked here. For less than a pound the kids can explore this old schooner and see a little of life aboard a sailing ship.

Near the ship you'll see the ruins of an old building, the opening for a large rose window still obvious in its west wall. The wall is 14th century, and the building it was a part of was even older—standing there even before the Norman Conquest. This was the grand *Palace of the Bishop of Winchester*, one of the most powerful medieval churchmen in England. Unfortunately, this association also has a more disreputable dimension: the good Bishop owned many of the local brothels, or at least collected the rents from the land on which the brothels stood. In fact, in early London, prostitutes were often referred to as "Winchester geese."

Walk down the street beside the palace wall. This is *Clink Street*. It got its name from the clanking of the chains of the men who were held in the foul and reeking prison here. Even in America we refer to a convict as being "in the clink."

At the west end of Clink Street you'll pass under a railway bridge and find one of London's most historic pubs, the *Anchor Bankside Tavern*. The present building is only 200 years old, but there has been an inn here much longer than that, and if you stop for lunch or other refreshment here, you are most certainly dining in precisely the same place Shakespeare often slaked his thirst.

The Anchor usually has a nice selection of hot and cold meat pies for lunch. If the weather is good, sit at one of the picnic tables overlooking the water and watch the river traffic go by.

Walk along Bankside and you'll pass the

> ***Tip:*** *Come back to the Anchor for a late supper one evening. It's inexpensive, and if you arrive shortly before dusk you can sit on the patio and watch the city come alight from the walkways of Tower Bridge to the grand dome of St. Paul's. It's one of the most marvelous sights you'll see in London.*

new *Globe Theatre* that we discussed in Chapter 10. The original location of the Globe, a block or so away on Park Street, is now marked with a great brass plaque on a fence which keeps visitors away from the actual site. But everyone probably will be fascinated by the names of the streets in the area. Bear Gardens Alley obviously was the location of a bear-baiting pit centuries ago. One street over is Cardinal Cap Alley, named for its association with noted churchmen. And on that street is a house which was the site of the Cardinal Hat, a well-known brothel in Shakespeare's day. Perhaps this would be a good place to leave Shakespeare's neighborhood and just continue a walk along the South Bank of the river, seeing the sights and shopping the markets.

Temple Bar and Fleet Street

Another historic area of London, one worth an hour or two some afternoon, is the Temple Bar area, the place where the City of London actually begins. (Remember the explanation in Chapter 2 about the difference between the City of London and the general London area.) The word *Bar* used to mean "gate," and it's still used that way in Scotland and the north of England.

Temple Bar is at the point where the Strand becomes Fleet Street, and the borough of Westminster becomes the City of London. It's called *Temple* Bar because it is also right at the entrance to the Middle Temple, one on the Inns of Court, home of London's legal establishment.

As you walk east on the Strand, you'll know when you've arrived at Temple Bar when you see a statue of Queen Victoria and a griffin, a mythological beast like a small dragon, in the middle of the street. The griffin is the symbol of the City of London, and you'll sometimes notice them as you pass the boundaries of the City in other places.

The City of London was and is the financial center of England, and wise monarchs have always been careful to stay on the good side of the people with money. The aldermen of the City always preferred to be left pretty much alone, so by ancient tradition, the king or queen of England was forbidden to enter the City without the invitation of the Lord Mayor, a tradition that is maintained to this day. When Queen Elizabeth attended the wedding of her own son, Prince Charles, in St. Paul's Cathedral, she was met at Temple Bar by the Lord Mayor and escorted up the street to the church. (That particular marriage, of course, is now history—but the tradition lives on.) Of course, Temple Bar was also one of the places the king used to put the severed heads of traitors on a spike to gaze down at the public.

As you stand at the entrance to the City you'll see some impressive-looking buildings nearby. On the south side of the street (your right if you're facing St. Paul's) is an old half-timbered Tudor building. This is one of the few buildings in London to survive the great fire of 1666. It was build in 1610 and would have been known to Shakespeare.

Upstairs is a small museum called Prince Henry's Room, which contains some interesting memorabilia of Samuel Pepys. It's probably not of much interest to the kids, but if anyone in your group *does* have a real interest in the history of the City, it's worth a half-hour.

Pepys was an interesting character. He kept a diary from 1660 to 1669 and recorded all the great events of the most tumultuous decade in London's history. He was a middle management government official who advanced rapidly. He was on the ship that carried

Charles II back from exile when the monarchy was restored in 1660. He was in London during the Plague of 1665. He watched the Great Fire from his backyard in 1666. And his diary records countless slice-of-life anecdotes that give an honest and wonderful picture of life during that period.

Right across the street is a huge Victorian building. Here are the Royal Courts of Justice. If you'd like to see the world's most widely-imitated criminal justice system in action, slip into a courtroom and watch the wigged and gowned judges and barristers at work for an hour. It's an interesting free show that will call to your mind all those Agatha Christie novels you've read and *Rumpole of the Bailey* TV shows you've watched.

At Temple Bar you've got a choice of two interesting strolls. Going straight ahead up Fleet Street will take you past the buildings that were once home to the world's greatest publishing industry. Now the newspapers have moved their operations to less congested areas. You'll go by St. Bride's Church (see Chapter 13) whose steeple formed the inspiration for the tiered wedding cake, and you'll end up after a leisurely 20 minutes at the steps of St. Paul's.

Before you get there, you might stop for lunch at another of London's most famous pubs, Ye Old Cheshire Cheese, on the north side of the street just before the traffic circle. This pub was supposedly the first building put up after the Great Fire, built for the convenience of the workmen who were rebuilding the City. It's widely considered to serve some of the best pub grub in London.

If you want a quieter walk, one away from the bustle of the traffic, go through the archway in that Tudor building and enter the Inns of Court. Suddenly everything is green and quiet. Here you may see the denizens of legal London scurrying by in their wigs and robes. Most important law firms have offices in one of the Inns of Court—the Inner and Middle Temple, Grey's Inn, and Lincoln's Inn. John Mortimer, the barrister who wrote the stories the *Rumpole* TV show was based on, has his offices in the Temple.

As you make your way among the buildings and gardens, be sure to stop at Temple Church, described in Chapter 13. The old part of the church was built in 1160 and is one of only three round churches in all of Britain. The effigies in the church mark the tombs of Crusaders.

Other Pageantry

If you're in London at the right time, there are a couple of annual events that display the pomp and ceremony we tourists love so much. In June is the *Queen's Birthday*, celebrated with the great spectacle *"Trooping the Colour"*. Actually Her Majesty was born in April, but the weather is better for a party in June. The celebration involves much ceremonial parading and marching about by assorted troops and regimental bands, and is truly a jolly good show. Tickets to the main portion of the show, which takes place in Horse Guards Parade off Whitehall, are tough to get, but there's lots to see as colorfully-uniformed troops parade in and out of the area.

In July or August is the *Royal Tournament* in Earl's Court in southwest London. Not a competition at all, but a series of military displays and demonstrations, the tournament also involves plenty of colorful costumes and pageantry. The tournament runs for a couple of weeks and tickets are plentiful, and some are inexpensive.

While short on ceremony, the *Livery Companies' Exhibition* in July is long on history and color. The Livery Companies, descendants of the old medieval guilds of tradesmen, still play an important role in the life of the City, although that role is more often philanthropic than commercial these days. Each July, the 100 companies sponsor a festival at London's 15th-century *Guildhall*, a short walk north from St. Paul's Cathedral. Members of many Companies wear their colorful medieval costumes and demonstrate ancient crafts of arrow making, stone carving, or clockmaking. The exhibition is free and includes admission to some parts of the ancient Guildhall not usually open to the public. For a very medieval feel, be sure to visit the building's crypt, where refreshments are served.

Colorful ethnic exhibitions and festivals take place most summer weekends in the courtyard behind the Church of St. Martin-in-the-Fields across from Trafalgar Square and the National Gallery. You'll

It's always polite to ask before you take a picture

find music, dancing, and a market which has both lovely handcrafted items and cheap London souvenirs. There are better places to do your shopping, but the entertainment is interesting and varied, and it provides a colorful alternative rest stop to sitting among the pigeons across the street.

Going to London without taking advantage of some of its rich history and local color is like going to the World Series and spending the whole game playing checkers under the bleachers. One of the best ways to soak up doses of history as you stroll the city is to watch for the Blue Plaques. Buildings where famous people have lived or where important events have taken place are awarded a blue plaque on the outside. The inscription describes what happened on the inside. There are hundreds of plaques and searching for them is a fun activity for everyone. They're located in every part of the city and offer many surprises. You might stumble across the neighborhood where Benjamin Franklin lived when he was ambassador from Pennsylvania Colony, or the house where television was first demonstrated, or the building where the Beatles gave their final rooftop concert. Few places have so rich a history as London, and nowhere is it more accessible.

Recommendations

✔ Spend a half day at the Tower. Nowhere in London is as rich in history and lore as this place.

✔ See the guard change somewhere once. More than once can be tedious, but the first time is fun. Take lots of pictures.

✔ Take a walk through a historical area and watch the Blue Plaques for familiar names. See Chapter 16 for more information on more interesting walks.

12. Music, Theatre, and Art

L ondon is one of the world's great culture capitals. Now
there's a word that's guaranteed to make most kids' eyes glaze
over! But culture comes in all shapes and sizes, and there are
plenty of opportunities for everyone to soak up culture and to have
a good time while doing it. Apart from the high quality of what's
available, much of it is inexpensive, even free.

As you can see from the title, we've divided this chapter into
three major categories, but before we get to them, we're going to
add a fourth, because we don't know quite where to put it, and
you're liable to find any of the other three represented here. We're
talking, of course, about London's famous street entertainers, the
buskers.

Buskers

Busking is centuries old, dating to the time when performers travelled from town to town to earn their living. You'll find buskers in
every corner of London, playing musical instruments, dancing,
juggling, sword fighting, drawing chalk masterpieces on the pavement, making pretty assistants disappear, and providing a constant
source of amusement for passersby.

Music, Theatre, and Art

Best places to find buskers are in Covent Garden or in front of the National Theatre on the South Bank near Waterloo. You'll certainly encounter them in the Underground, though they're not supposed to be there. The police usually leave them alone, though, unless they get too loud or get in the way. While you'll see your share of thin-voiced guitar plunkers with more optimism than talent, you will also find high quality, professional-level performers.

Street musicians playing Brahms in front of a Covent Garden pub

Buskers earn their pay from the generosity of their audiences. If you just walk on by, there's no need to tip a performer. But if you stop to watch the act or to take pictures, it's only fair to drop some money in the guitar case or hat that you'll undoubtedly find sitting on the sidewalk. There's no fixed amount to contribute. If you just watch for a minute or two, 20p is fair. Longer might warrant 50p, and if you stay for an entire 20-minute magic show, a pound or two would not be misplaced.

Don't be shy if you're asked to be part of the act. One of the Lains was once drafted as a magician's assistant; another served as a second to a duelist. It's great fun and you really won't look foolish: it's in the performer's interest to send everybody away happy. Besides . . . you'll never see these people again in your life. Enjoy it!

Music

You can hear some of the world's greatest musicians in London, of course. The Royal Opera House is in Covent Garden (although it's currently undergoing extensive renovations) and symphony orchestras play at the South Bank Center and the Barbican. But that's probably not the sort of music you're looking for on a family vacation. Most kids would rather hear something a little more modern, and most parents would rather hear something cheaper. We can help.

Cheap—Even Free!—Music

You're apt to stumble onto music almost anywhere. Wandering through St. Paul's one afternoon we were certain we heard a band somewhere. We had. When we left we discovered the London Transport Band playing a concert on the steps of the cathedral. We sat on the steps and enjoyed it for 20 minutes, then went on our way.

One of our favorite ways to spend a summer Sunday is with a picnic lunch and a stack of Sunday papers in Hyde Park. We take a position just northwest of the Serpentine, where we can listen to the music from the Jazz Brunch at the restaurant. About the time that's over, there's a Sunday afternoon concert at the bandshell just off in the opposite direction. Can't beat the atmosphere—or the price!

In Chapter 4 we advised you to make a copy of *Time Out* magazine one of your first purchases. Here's where it begins to pay for itself. The magazine lists much of the entertainment going on in London each week, along with locations and prices. The music

Music, Theatre, and Art

section is broken into four categories: Rock, Country & Folk, Jazz, and Classical, with some subcategories. If you feel like listening to music, there are few places that offer better opportunities. And much of the music is free! See the sidebar on this page for more details. You might not have come to London specifically for the music, but you'll find it everywhere, and chances are, it will cost you next to nothing.

Other Music-Related Sites

Rock Circus (*London Pavilion at Piccadilly Circus, admission charge*) has been called "Madam Tussaud's with a light show." In fact, that's pretty accurate. It *is* run by Madam Tussaud's, but instead of presenting wax figures of world leaders, monarchs, and criminals, it presents

---

Music in the Air

We saved our copy of Time Out *from one recent trip and here's what we found for one typical week in June:*

There were 800 musical events listed for the week. Rock music accounted for 48 percent of the events, Jazz for 29 percent, Country and Folk for 15 percent, and Classical for 8 percent. We also saw plenty of music that wasn't listed; the London Transport Band on the steps of St. Paul's was one. Lunchtime concerts in churches are common all over the city and aren't always well publicized. You could easily choose from a thousand musical events in London every week.

Prices cover a wide range, but unless you buy tickets for U2 at Wembley Stadium, they're unlikely to put a hole in your budget. Of the 800 events listed in Time Out *for the week in question, about 12 percent did not list a price. The ones that did broke down this way:*

Free — —	*31 percent*
Less than £2 —	*10 percent*
£2 to £5—	*44 percent*
£6 to £10—	*11 percent*
More than £10 —	*4 percent*

Many of the free events were in pubs, but children 14 and over are welcome there, and those are often good places to hear Celtic folk music and jazz. Music is accessible all over London, and you don't have to plan too carefully unless there's something you especially want to see: you'll stumble

the history of pop music from the 1950s to the present. It may not be the parents' cup of tea (although it may provoke a bit of high-school-years nostalgia) but it might be a treat for the young rockers in the family. The **Guinness World of Records** (Chapter 11)

> *across it in unlikely places. Probably the most unusual musical experience we've had came from the sound of bagpipes outside our flat in Pimlico early one evening. We investigated and found a piper in full kit standing on the sidewalk across the street, a few doors down, tooting vigorously. We listened to his 15-minute concert then discovered that he had been sent to welcome home a newlywed couple living nearby. His little concert was not listed by Time Out.*

is nearby for family members who don't want to Rock & Roll.

In Chapter 15 we'll remind you about London's three huge record stores: **Tower Records** in Piccadilly Circus and the **Virgin Records Megastore** and **HMV Records**, both on Oxford Street (*Tube: Marble Arch: Central line*). If you can't find the records you're looking for in one of those places, finding them may be hopeless.

If you'd like to have your picture taken in the same crosswalk as the Beatles did on the cover of their *Abbey Road* album, it's perfectly possible, if you don't mind the possibility of getting run over. *Abbey Road* is in northwest London. Take the Metropolitan line to St. John's Wood. Abbey Road is about two blocks west of the Underground station. Be careful, though. Even though motorists are used to dodging tourists here, it's a busy street and London drivers are not noted for their patience or their courtesy.

Theatre

The theatre scene in New York is impressive . . . until you get to London. If you enjoy live theatre, you've reached the pinnacle; there's nothing else like it in the world. Just as New York City offers Broadway and Off-Broadway theater, London has *West End* and *Fringe* theatre. We'll tell you a little about each and make some suggestions.

Your family might enjoy a visit to the Globe Theatre

West End Theatre

Like New York's Broadway, but more so. As this chapter was being written, there were 58 shows running in the West End. The variety is staggering. There are old warhorses like Agatha Christie's *The Mousetrap*, which opened in 1951 and is still going strong; blockbuster shows like *Miss Saigon* and *Les Miserables*; revivals of popular shows like *Oliver!* and *A Chorus Line*; several Shakespeare plays; serious dramas by Ibsen and Tennessee Williams; comedies, musicals, thrillers, children's shows, dramas—every imaginable theatrical genre.

Tickets are almost always available and prices are significantly less than for Broadway shows. Orchestra seats for popular shows on Broadway were $65 to $70 last time we were there. West End prices top out at less than £30, or about $48 for equivalent seats (the "stalls"). But there are ways to do even better.

Best bet is to go to Leicester Square, home of the *Half-Price Ticket Booth* run by the Society of London Theatre. Here, leftover tickets are sold for day-of-performance shows for half their face value, plus a small service charge. Tickets for the blockbuster shows won't be found here, but almost everything else will: on a typical day there tells y___ __d to know a__ __nis booth. *Don't* buy from ticket touts around the area. You'll be overcharged and perhaps sold bogus tickets. If you want to see one of the shows not available from the booth, go to the box office. You'll get genuine tickets, will pay no more than face value, and probably will get better seats.

Unsold tickets and returns are often available at the theatre 30 to 60 minutes before showtime. Telephone the theatre to see if they offer tickets like that and, if so, who may buy them. Sometimes those offers are limited to students, but often they are not. You could find yourself getting a £25 seat for £5 or £10 if you're

London's Theatre Lineup

The Society of London Theatre operates a half-price ticket booth in Leicester Square for seats on the day of performance. The booth opens at 12:30 to sell tickets for matinees and for evening shows. The names of the shows available each day are posted on a board outside the booth, and are removed as soon as each show is sold out.

Best strategy is to make a list of the shows your family would like to see and put them in order of priority. Don't expect to get discount tickets to the famous blockbusters like Cats or Phantom, but otherwise most shows have leftover tickets available here. A complete list of shows can be found in the brochure available in cartons outside the booth as well as in most hotels and tourist-oriented pamphlet racks. Time Out magazine also carries a complete list of shows and capsule descriptions and reviews. The Sunday papers also cover the West End thoroughly.

When you've picked out several shows you'd like to see, join the queue in Leicester Square. It's a long line, but moves surprisingly fast. There's always good conversation with the people around you, sometimes almost a carnival atmosphere, and your wait passes quickly. One person can take line duty while the others browse through the many shops that surround the square.

When you reach the front of the queue, tell the person at the window what show you want and how many seats you need. Prices are 50 percent of the ticket value, plus a £2 service charge. Note that these are cash only sales. Credit cards and traveller's cheques are not accepted.

lucky. The downside of that, of course, is that sometimes there are no tickets available, and you won't know until just before the show. If you're flexible and want to take the chance, you can often get a terrific bargain. The seats might not be in the stalls, but "dress circle" (mezzanine) seats are excellent, and even balcony seats are usually better than balcony seats on Broadway, since theatres tend to be smaller.

Even though it's not in the theatre district, one of London's most pleasant and popular West End venues is the **Open Air Theatre** in Regent's Park *(Tube: Regent's Park—Bakerloo Line; or Baker Street, where 5 lines cross)*. Set between a grove of trees and Queen Mary's Rose Garden, it's a wonderful place to spend a warm summer evening. The plays are produced by the New Shakespeare Company, which performs three shows in repertory. One is usually *A Midsummer Night's Dream*, the perfect Shakespeare play for a midsummer night in London. The other shows are normally another Shakespeare comedy or familiar tragedy and a musical. The shows change every week or two in rotation throughout the summer. There's a barbecue next to the theatre and food and drink served inside, and if the night turns chilly you can even rent a shawl or blanket. We've enjoyed taking a picnic supper to dine among the roses before the show. Watching Shakespeare in a leafy

This is a good time to get reacquainted with Shakespeare

park, under the open sky as it was originally performed, seems like the perfect thing to do in London, even if the jets flying into Heathrow do occasionally muffle the dialogue.

Fringe Theatre

Fringe shows run a broad range from plays in an upstairs room of a pub to theatres almost indistinguishable from those in the West End. Prices run anywhere from £1 to £15. Last trip we saw a one-man Dickens show in the library of the Dickens House Museum and an uproariously funny comedy spoof of the royal family at a nice neighborhood theatre in South Kensington (a show which two months later moved to the West End with tickets three times as costly).

The best place to get information about fringe shows is from our old friend *Time Out*. (And no, they're not underwriting this book. It's just the essential guide to entertainment in London.) A recent list of fringe shows totaled 101, with a range of types including everything you'd see in the West End, and lots more—experimental works, new plays, student-written shows, political statements: you have to read the descriptions in the listings to get the full effect.

Fringe shows can be directed at children or they can be racier or more graphic than what you'd see in the West End, so unless it's a play you're familiar with, you might want to phone ahead to see if it's suitable for families. In fact, phoning ahead is always a good idea for fringe shows. Some of the theatres seat as few as a dozen people and booking—making reservations—is essential.

If you're in London during December, go to the *Pantomimes*, delightful family-oriented shows, not really performed in mime, retelling many favorite stories and fairy tales.

Just for Kids

Here are a few more places to consider if you have younger children.

The **Unicorn Theatre for Children** (*6–7 Great Newport Street, WC2. Tube: Covent Garden—Piccadilly line*) produces shows especially for children in the afternoons, especially on weekends. The **Little Angel Theatre** *(14 Dagmar Passage, N1. Tube: Angel—Northern line)* near Camden Passage Market is one of the few permanent puppet theatres in Britain. Their Saturday morning performances are extremely popular with younger children. Despite its name, the **Polka Children's Theatre** *(240 The Broadway, Wimbledon. Tube: Wimbledon—District line)* has nothing to do with folkdancing. The theatre puts on live and puppet plays for children, conducts workshops in many aspects of the arts, and is a pleasant place to get away from the tourists and meet the in-the-know local families whose children come here.

Art

Young children would often prefer to go to bed without supper than to spend an hour in an art museum, but older children and parents might enjoy going. It seems like London has as many art galleries as Chinese restaurants (and it has a lot of those!) and some of the best are the small, very specialized galleries. Here, though, we'll profile four of the best-known museums, then tell you about our favorite place for art.

Four World-Class Galleries

If you took our walking tour in Chapter 6 you've already seen two of the great art museums of London, the **National Gallery of Art** and the **National Portrait Gallery** alongside Trafalgar Square. There is no admission charge for either, and the collections are world renowned. The National Gallery has one of the world's few paintings by Leonardo, a breathtaking collection of Renaissance works and European masters, and much more. The National Portrait Gallery displays its paintings chronologically according to when the subject lived. Begin on the top floor with paintings of the early monarchs of England and work your way down to modern times. In both galleries you'll recognize many paintings you've seen reproduced in books, usually a fun realization for children. *("Hey, Mom! That picture of Henry VIII is in my history book!")*

If you like French Impressionists, start from Trafalgar Square and take a fifteen-minute stroll up the Strand, once the chief street leading from Westminster into the City, until you reach the **Courtauld Institute**. Here is London's best collection of Impressionist and Post-Impressionist paintings. There is an admission charge for this gallery, so non-enthusiasts might wander down the Strand toward Fleet Street and the City while the art aficionadi spend an hour at the Courtauld.

The **Tate Gallery** (*Millbank, SW1: free admission. Tube: Pimlico—Victoria line*) is often more appealing to young people because it houses the national collection of 20th-century art, which is frequently a good deal less conventional than the Old Masters. The Tate also has the most extensive collection of works by British artists.

A Walk in the Park

When your family is tired of looking at art by dead people, it's fun to check out some live ones. So head off to Hyde Park on a Sunday. As you stroll the mile-long stretch of Bayswater Road that runs along the north side of the park, you'll see the works of hundreds of local artists for sale—painters, mostly, but also sculptors, metalworkers, weavers, practitioners of a dozen kinds of art.

Their works are for sale and make a special memento of your trip or lovely gift for someone back home, and it's easy to strike up a conversation with the artist, who is certainly from London or somewhere nearby. But there's never any pressure to buy; it's a public sidewalk and you're free to stroll or stop to look as much as you please. If you've been picnicking in the park, listening to the music we told you about at the beginning of this chapter, here's an equally relaxed way to close your day.

Recommendations

✔ London is the world's theatre capital, so take in a show—West End, fringe, or children's.

Music, Theatre, and Art

✔ At least cherry-pick a few of the great works at the National Gallery: Leonardo, Michelangelo, and Rembrandt. There are few places in the world where it's possible for your children to see these masters together.

✔ Don't forget your copy of *Time Out* when you're looking for activities.

For the latest updates to *London for Families*,
check our page on the World Wide Web at

http://www.as.udayton.edu/com/faculty/lain/lonfam.htm

13. Churches, Bridges, and Other Grand Structures

L ondon suffered terrible bomb damage during World War II;
entire sections of the city were destroyed. But through the
vigilance of its citizens, and miracles great and small, many
of London's grandest buildings survived either intact or in a repara-
ble state. In this chapter we'll suggest the great edifices most likely
to capture the fancy of someone in your family. In deference to the
position of the monarchy, let's start with the royal residences.

Palaces

Some we've already discussed. In Chapter 11 we talked a bit about
Buckingham Palace and its pricey tour. The appearance of Buck
House (as the royals supposedly call it) is often disappointing to
tourists who find its architecture insufficiently grand. **Kensington
Palace**, at the far west end of Hyde Park/Kensington Gardens, is
little better, although admission to its state apartments is less expensive and includes an interesting exhibit of court dress over the
past three centuries.

If you want to see a royal palace that really *looks* like what a royal palace should look like, try **St. James's Palace**, just north of the Mall near Buckingham Palace. It's a grand old complex and even though royalty hasn't lived here for centuries it is still the official diplomatic center of Britain: foreign ambassadors are still accredited to "The Court of St. James's." Unfortunately, St. James's Palace is not open to the public. Its chapel is open to the public for Sunday morning services from October until the Sunday before Easter. After watching the Changing of the Guard, it's worth a walk back in that direction to see the palace from the outside, at least. The more gruesome-minded members of your party will enjoy the fact that this residence of kings is build on a site that once held an asylum for female lepers.

Churches

London is a city of churches. Every corner of the city holds historic and architecturally interesting houses of worship, but there are two in particular that you will want to see: Westminster Abbey and St. Paul's Cathedral.

Westminster Abbey

We came past here in our walk in Chapter 6; now it's time to go inside for an awe-inspiring tour of this, the most important church in Britain. People have been worshipping here for at least 1,500 years and probably longer. The present church was built, like most grand cathedrals, in stages over several hundred years. It was begun by King Edward the Confessor, who was later canonized a saint, and dedicated in 1065, but its essentials now date mostly from the 13th century. Edward's tomb in the royal chapels is considered the holiest spot in England.

There is no charge to enter the nave of the church, which is humbling and beautiful, but which is always crowded with tourists. Walk about and admire the burial inscriptions and ornamentation. The *Tomb of the Unknown Warrior* is just inside the Great West

Door, a spot treated with the same reverence as America's Tomb of the Unknowns at Arlington National Cemetery. About halfway along the north side of the nave, look for the grave of the poet Ben Jonson, a contemporary of Shakespeare, in the floor. It is a small slab, supposedly because Jonson died poor and could afford nothing more, so he was buried standing up! As a final insult, his name is misspelled *Johnson* on his stone.

The choir screen separates the nave from what are called here the Royal Chapels, the greater body of the church. The screen was common in most such Gothic cathedrals, the choir and sanctuary being reserved for the vowed religious. Sir Isaac Newton is buried just in front of the screen.

There is a charge of about £4 to enter the Royal Chapels. Pay it! (Student discounts are available.) Here are buried the great of England. You will find dozens of its kings, queens, and nobles, including St. Edward, Queen Elizabeth I and her hated sister Queen Mary ("Bloody Mary"), Mary Queen of Scots, and countless others.

This part of the abbey is where every king and queen of England, except two, has been crowned since William the Conqueror in 1066, and you can walk up the same aisle as each of those monarchs. The Coronation Chair, a rude wooden chair that is centuries old, is used only for newly-crowned monarchs. Beneath it for centuries rested the Stone of Scone, symbol of Scottish sovereignty, brought from (or stolen from, depending on your political persuasion) Scotland in 1297. (To head off increasing support for Scottish nationalists, prime minister John Major returned the Stone to Scotland in November 1996.)

Don't miss the Henry VII Chapel! Its intricately carved woodwork and the ceiling stonework delicate as fine lace are heart-stoppingly beautiful, and the colorful banners of the Knights of the Bath, one of England's chief orders of chivalry, add to the ancient splendor. This single room is worth going to England for.

Poet's Corner is worth wandering around for a little while. Chaucer is buried here and there are graves and monuments for all the greats of English literature; even some Americans are memorialized. The list reads like the index in your child's lit book.

A guided tour from one of the priests or vergers of the Abbey is available at a bit more than the cost of admission to the Royal Chapels, and provides much of the history and traditions of the church. It also includes admission to a couple of other sites in the complex. If you don't want to spend money on the guided tour, however, you can pick up a free brochure when you enter the Royal Chapels that will give you the essential information you need to understand what you're seeing.

Westminster Abbey is not open for sightseeing on Sundays.

St. Paul's Cathedral

If pressed, priests at the Abbey and at St. Paul's will admit that there's a bit of a rivalry between the churches. The Abbey's ecclesias-

> ***Tip:*** *In Westminster Abbey everyone enjoys making a brass rubbing as a souvenir or gift. Visitors are no longer permitted to make rubbings of the actual memorials, but many are reproduced and available in the Cloisters. For a small fee, staff will supply the materials and a child can create a unique memento in ten minutes or so.*

tical nose was just a little out of joint when Charles and Diana chose to be married at St. Paul's although perhaps that rift was eased after the funeral of the princess in the Abbey in 1997.

Both are splendid churches, but in very different ways. Westminster is all towering Gothic grandeur while St. Paul's is Renaissance majesty overlaid with the ornateness of the Victorian age. Honestly there's no reason for them to compete; they're as different as apples and eggs.

St. Paul's is the centerpiece of the City. When London was destroyed by fire in 1666, the blaze took with it an even larger, taller Gothic version of St. Paul's, and the loss was devastating to an already-shattered city. The rebuilding of an even grander St. Paul's was the greatest achievement of Christopher Wren, who also rebuilt dozens of the City's smaller churches. In the 19th century the Victorians, always big fans of intricate, even garish, decoration, enhanced the great cathedral with tons of gold.

The church is done on a vast scale and is the third largest in the world, trailing only St. Peter's in Rome and St. Isaac's in St. Petersburg, Russia. Its magnificent dome, although no longer the City's tallest point, reaches 365 feet, and for those with the energy to climb its 530 steps (probably the kids), affords a stunning view of London. Even if you can't make it all the way to the top (the last bit is cramped and a little scary), it's worth paying £1 to climb the 259 steps to the Whispering Gallery at the base of the dome. Kids invariably enjoy the experiences of carrying on soft conversations with people more than 120 feet away.

Don't miss the crypt. Here are the gravesites of Britain's greatest military heros, Lord Nelson and the Duke of Wellington, and the graves or memorials of numerous great artists and medical pioneers, as well as, fittingly enough, the grave of Christopher Wren himself.

There is a £2 admission charge to St. Paul's (children are less) except for services. The church is open seven days a week but sightseeing is discouraged during services.

Other Churches

As you walk about London, stop in and see the churches you pass. Most have interesting histories and no two are alike architecturally. Even the younger members of your family might like to see the floor of a Roman temple visible in **St. Bride's** crypt (*Fleet Street*). In any case, its famous steeple was supposedly the inspiration for the multi-tiered cake traditional at weddings. This church is called the Printers' Cathedral because of its centuries-long association with the newspapers and publishing houses that used to line Fleet Street, and its crypt also contains an informative exhibit on the history of publishing.

Would someone enjoy seeing the effigies of slain crusaders in full armor? Visit **Temple Church**, a unique 800-year-old round church in the Inns of Court (*Tube: Temple—District, and Circle lines*) mentioned in the last chapter. Observe the penitential cell built into the wall, where during the Middle Ages at least one member of the

Knights Templar was imprisoned until he starved to death.

Westminster Cathedral *(Ashley Place, SW1: Tube: Victoria—Circle, District, and Victoria lines)* is the chief Roman Catholic church in England, and is a striking early 20th-century structure. Its 273-foot-high bell tower affords a stunning view of the West End, and best of all, it has an elevator and is free.

One of the great pleasures of London is just wandering through the city. As you do, stop and visit the many churches you pass. They have interesting and unique histories and can be a small refuge of quiet in the midst of a busy day of sightseeing. The history of London is closely allied with that of its churches. You're certain to find them worth your time regardless of your family's religious orientation.

Bridges

The Romans threw the first wooden bridge across the lower Thames about 19 centuries ago near the site of modern London Bridge. A stone bridge was finished about the year 1200, and it survived more than 600 years. The current London bridge, the third on the site, opened in 1973 and is an uninteresting, rather generic bridge. But there are two others you want to see.

Bridges may be grand . . . or not so grand

Westminster Bridge

The view from this bridge is one of London's most wonderful pieces of eye candy, offering a picture-book view of the Houses of Parliament, Big Ben, the River Thames, the stately offices of Whitehall, the old London County Council building, and much more. You *will* get a memorable photograph from this spot, and it's an ideal place to ask a passerby to take a picture of your whole family together with this scene as the backdrop. Don't be shy about asking someone: it happens hundreds, maybe thousands, of times a day on this bridge.

Tower Bridge

In the early 1970s an American entrepreneur bought London Bridge, which was being replaced, and had it shipped to Arizona as a tourist attraction. When it arrived and they reassembled it, he realized he'd bought the wrong bridge: *This* is the one he really wanted. This great marvel of Victorian engineering is, with the Big Ben tower and St. Paul's dome, the third of London's great visual landmarks. Its great drawbridge mechanism is now operated by electricity instead of the original steam, and the bridge is raised several times a day (it takes just 90 seconds), much to the dismay of motorists. You can take an excellent but relatively expensive tour of the bridge and its inner workings, but family discounts are available and the views up and down the river from the walkways are memorable.

Other Grand Structures

It's impossible to list all the great sights that have broad family appeal. That's why involving everyone in the planning is so important: There are so many possibilities that some exciting things will have to get left out. The trick is to find the things that are most exciting to *your* family. Here are three more to consider:

Tower Bridge opens several times a day to let ships pass through

Houses of Parliament

We've been past here on our walk in Chapter 6, gazed at it from the bridge in this chapter, and spotted it from afar from all over town, so it's time to dedicate a few paragraphs to the distinctive **Houses of Parliament**.

Parliament began meeting on this site in 1275, and there has been a succession of buildings here. The last one burned down in 1834 and a competition was held to design a new one. This was the winner. (To see one of the ones that didn't win, go to St. Pancras railway station on Euston Road and see the old St. Pancras Hotel. A losing entry in the Parliament competition was recycled into that magnificent but overwrought edifice.) The best view of the Parliament is from across the river, along the Albert Embankment. The effect is spectacular at night, when the building is lit dramatically.

For a view inside, there are two possibilities. You can arrange for a guided tour through the American Embassy or from a Member of Parliament, should you happen to meet one, or you can join the line each afternoon at St. Stephen's entrance (facing the rear of Westminster Abbey). Visitors are admitted at about 4:30 each afternoon, but the queue can be lengthy and you might easily wait an hour or two.

Once inside you can sit in the visitors' gallery of either the House of Commons or the House of Lords and listen to the debates, just as you can when visiting the U.S. Congress in Washington. The chambers, especially the opulent House of Lords, are worth the wait for interested adults, but even older children may find the wait tedious. We think the wait is worth the trouble of seeing one of the world's oldest democratic institutions in action, even if the debate is nothing meaningful to us. (Last time we were there, the Commons was discussing fisheries and the members of Lords who were awake were debating historic preservation.) The inside of the building reflects the grandeur of the once-great British Empire, however, and is as awe-inspiring for British schoolchildren as a visit to the Capitol is for Americans.

> ***Tip:*** *Parliament usually sits until late in the evening, so seek entrance after 6 p.m. The line will be much shorter, and may be gone entirely.*

The Monument

In a city filled with monuments, there is only one *The* Monument. First, a little history. As centuries go, England had an especially bad 17th. There was quite a lot of religious strife in the early 1600s, with the crown being passsed back and forth between those sympathetic to the Catholic Church and those who were firmly Protestant. In the 1640s there was civil war between supporters of the king and supporters of Parliament, largely ending in 1648 when the king, Charles I, got his head lopped off. Twelve years later in 1660 the monarchy was restored under the dead king's son, Charles II. But that was only the beginning of the worst decade in London's history.

In 1665 a terrible outbreak of the plague wiped out entire parishes in London. At least a hundred thousand people died, but no one knows the exact total. A substantial percentage of the population of the city was wiped out.

It got worse in 1666. Early one September morning a fire broke out in a baker's shop in Pudding Lane. By the time it died out three days later, virtually the entire city had been burned to the ground. Few people lost their lives this time, but almost nothing was left standing in the entire square mile.

The Monument was erected 30 years later as a memorial to the fire. It was designed by (who else!) Christopher Wren. It is exactly 202 feet tall and stands the same distance, 202 feet, from the spot the fire started.

Since we've already sent the kids to the dome of St. Paul's, the bell tower of Westminster Cathedral, and the walkway of Tower Bridge, we might as well have them climb the 311-step twisted staircase to see the view from here, too, and take pictures for those on the ground too timid or too tired to see it for themselves. The view is, like the others, well worth the climb. What they'll enjoy even more is the chance to tease the ones who felt too weary or too old to make the climb. Let 'em rub it in a little.

The Roman Wall

Britain was a province of Rome for almost twice as long as the United States has been a country, and there are examples of Roman occupation all over the island. Major roads, including principal London streets, follow the old Roman roads, and Roman coins and artifacts are abundant and inexpensive in the markets. The most lasting souvenirs from Rome's rule, though, are several sections of the wall they built for the defense of the city.

If you take the tube to the Tower of London you'll see the most impressive remaining fragment of the wall, standing just outside the Tower Hill Underground station. There's a smaller fragment inside the Tower, but starting from the section at the tube station

One of the very first tourists

you can take a two-mile walk, marked with plaques that point out places of special interest, that follows the path of the wall. In several places fragments of the wall are visible, as are some ruins from an even older Roman fort. The Wall Walk ends at the Museum of London, located, appropriately enough, on the street called London Wall.

Kids often don't care about just looking at buildings—it's too passive an activity. But London has hundreds of buildings worth looking at and chances are they'll find themselves as enraptured by the sight of many of these places as their parents are. And if standing around looking at buildings isn't active enough for one of them, well, there are almost always stairs to climb for a great view that only the young and vigorous can enjoy.

Recommendations

✔ Visit Westminster Abbey and St. Paul's Cathedral, but do it on different days so the majesty of one doesn't detract from the splendor of the other. Look into other churches that you pass on your wanderings.

Churches, Bridges, and Other Grand Structures

✔ If there's time, visit Parliament.

✔ Take advantage of (and photographs from!) some of the birds-eye view spots. It will be a high point of your trip.

14. Parks and Diversions

In almost every chapter we've mentioned attractions in and around London's expansive parks. Few other cities in the world boast of such a well developed and maintained network of green space.

The showplaces are the large Royal Parks, often called the "Lungs of London." These parks (Regent's, Hyde, Green, St. James's, Greenwich, and Kensington Gardens) were for the most part once private hunting preserves for the king and his cronies or were the grounds of royal palaces. Now they are wonderful public havens from the grit and noise of the big city. They are well used by both tourists and locals, and combined with London's other parks and squares, as well as its other recreational opportunities, you have an almost limitless number of ways to unwind from the bustle of "touristing."

The Royal Parks

Each of the Royal Parks has an individual character. Visit each once, then be returned blindfolded to one of them at random and you'd know almost instantly where you were. They're as different as Westminster Abbey and St. Paul's from each other, but while like great churches they have similarities, each has its own unique

Parks and Diversions

Speakers Corner is always interesting

elements that make it notable, just as the great churches do.

Regent's Park has the London Zoo, Queen Mary's Rose Garden, the Open Air Theatre, and the canals. At the west end is the striking London Central Mosque. Within and around the park are numerous impressive 18th- and 19th-century mansions. Regent's Park also has what must be the tamest squirrels in London.

For the best free show in London, go to **Hyde Park** on a Sunday. We've already told you to picnic there, listen to the music, and see the artists along the north side. Here's one more reason: near Marble Arch (originally designed as an entrance for Buckingham Palace) is **Speakers' Corner**. This famous bastion of free speech attracts dozens of speakers and hundreds of spectators every Sunday of the year. Things really get going around noon, with true believers of every political, social, and religious persuasion standing on stepladders and overturned milk crates, haranguing anyone who will listen to their views. On any given Sunday you'll listen to aging socialists, free sex advocates, feminists and male supremacists, conservative and liberal Christians, angry blacks, angry whites, patriots, monarchists and those who would send the royal family packing. *Anyone* can get "up on a soapbox" about anything here, and they certainly do. The most interesting speakers have the largest crowds around them. If you or a member of your party is feeling particularly outspoken and brave, go right ahead and start speaking. You may get heckled, but that's part of the fun.

For all the heated debate, things *never* get out of hand. The police, while never entirely out of sight, are two or three hundred yards away from the action and never interfere. Even the most acrimonious debates are quite civil; speaker and heckler may exchange barbs and insults for half an hour, and when the speaker packs up his ladder and literature to go, the heckler will help him load it in the boot of his car.

The hecklers are as much a part of the show as the speakers, jumping gleefully on any lapses in the logic of a speaker's argument, and defending themselves in turn from attack by the speaker or by other hecklers. (Look especially for a 30-ish doughy-faced man, often in a baseball or cricket cap, who for several years has been acknowledged as the heckler's heckler.)

Kids always like to feed the birds at Hyde Park

Parks and Diversions

There's much else to see in Hyde Park. Don't be surprised to see teenagers playing baseball (usually not at all well!) or Londoners exercising their horses along the road called the Ring, or along Rotten Row, once a popular spot for duels.

Hyde Park gives way to **Kensington Gardens** once you cross the Serpentine. Look for the statue of Peter Pan as you walk toward the lovely Italian Gardens. There's a playground for children in the northwest corner of Kensington Gardens. Focus of this park, of course, is Kensington Palace.

Green Park and **St. James's Park** are much smaller and have fewer notable attractions, but closer associations with royalty. Buckingham Palace sits in a corner of Green Park, and St. James's Palace overlooks the park of the same name. These are where the kings and queens of the realm have taken their leisure and where (behind a high-walled part of Green Park) the Queen still walks with her grandchildren and her corgis.

In Chapter 17 we'll take you down the river to Greenwich, but for now, we'll include **Greenwich Park** among its royal cousins. It is the oldest of the Royal Parks and is capped by the Old Royal Observatory, originator of Greenwich Mean Time and the Prime Meridian, the base points for our modern measures of time and geography. We'll return to Greenwich later.

Feel free to relax in one of the deck chairs that dot the open areas of the parks, but if you do, be prepared to give 50p to the concessionaire who cares for them. He'll come by at intervals to collect. If you feel like exercising instead of lounging, you can hire a bicycle or rowboat at Hyde Park or Regent's Park. Inquire at the boathouse near the pond.

Other Green Space

London is home to countless other parks and squares. Some of the largest are **Holland Park** (near Kensington Gardens), **Russell Square** (near the British Museum), and **Grosvenor Square** (near the American Embassy east of Hyde Park). These are supplemented by smaller squares in every neighborhood. You're apt to meet the local residents here walking their dogs or watching their children, always good excuses to strike up a conversation.

Our vote for the park with the best view is **Tower Bridge Park**. In other ways it's less comfortable than most of the others because there are no mature trees and amenities are limited. It is absolutely the best place to take a photograph of Tower Bridge, though; you can't avoid getting a memorable shot from this vantage point. It's an uncrowded place that sees far more locals than tourists, most of whom seldom cross the river here.

For a daylong excursion to the park, try **Hampstead Heath**, a huge park four miles north of central London. You can get there on the tube. Take the Northern line (Edgeware branch) to the picturesque village of Hampstead and enter the Heath from the south, or stay on until the next stop at Golders Green on its north side. There are miles of easy hiking trails there, a large children's playground, duck ponds, even swimming beaches, called bathing ponds. (In fact there are three: one for men only, and one for women—well separated by a boating pond—and one for mixed bathing.) The poet Keats had a house here, as did a number of other notables of English literature. There are outdoor concerts of classical music on summer Saturday evenings at Kenwood House in the park, and bicycles and boats for hire. Hampstead Heath is the perfect place to spend a day letting the kids run off the energy built up by doing too much standing and slow walking in museums.

For a nature excursion that's just a little different—and this is going to sound strange—take your family to the cemetery! Near Hampstead is **Highgate** (*Tube: Northern line, High Barnet branch*) whose famous cemetery is an odd but well-known tourist attraction in itself. Everyone will marvel at the fantastic monuments and curious inscriptions to be found down every winding lane. The most famous permanent resident of Highgate is Karl Marx, who was buried here in 1883. The novelist Mary Ann Evans, a.k.a. George Eliot, also found her last resting place here.

Parks and Diversions

Two More Outings

If you have time to really savor the English experience, we have a couple of other suggestions at hand that may appeal to some members of your family. These may not be everyone's cup of tea, but they'll give everyone a tale or two to carry with them back to school or work.

Take in a Cricket or Football Match

If you have a sports fan in your house, this is a good bet for a fun afternoon. Seems like half of all American kids play soccer these days, so going to a soccer match (the British, like most of the world, call it *football*) will spark an interest. There are big-league matches between some of the world's top professional teams, as well as school and amateur matches, almost every day in the fall and winter. Don't try to figure out the schedule from the newspaper sports page. Check your copy of *Time Out*. It will list all the matches and directions for getting there. Note that British soccer fans can be drunken and rowdy at times; their fans have even been banned from attending European matches in the past. Local and amateur matches should pose no trouble at all and you're unlikely to be able to get tickets for big international matches anyway.

For a very different afternoon, try the genteel game of cricket. Despite what you have heard, it's *not* a boring game, but a very leisurely and subtle one—so leisurely and subtle that it's easy for the uninitiated to mistake it for boring! We won't try to give you all the rules, but it's easy to see baseball's origins in the game. The basic idea is for the batter to hit the ball and run to the opposite base, passing a teammate who runs from the other base at the same time. Each time they cross they score a run for their team. When the batter hits the ball he can choose whether or not to run, depending on whether he thinks he and his teammate can make it safely to the opposite bases.

The defensive team, on the other hand, tries to put the batter or other runner out by catching the ball in the air (so cricket batsmen usually try to hit the ball on the ground), or by knocking over the sticks (wickets) at one of the bases before a runner can get there, or in one of several other ways. There's more to it than that, of course, but those are the main ideas and give you enough to start with.

There are two chief places to watch cricket. **Lord's Cricket Ground**, near Regent's Park, is the Yankee Stadium and Cooperstown of cricket in one, its most hallowed ground. **The Oval**, near the Imperial War Museum, is the other great stadium. There are matches at one or the other most days in summer and admission usually will be £5 or less. Don't try to go to one of the big international "test" matches unless you're a real fan. They're expensive and hard to get seats for.

Don't feel like you have to stay for the whole match. It will last all day, or more. Go for a couple of hours, sit in the sunshine and relax, and let the man and his son sitting next to you explain to their American cousins (you!) the intricacies of this old game.

Go to Tea

If there's anything more English than going to a cricket match, it would have to be "taking tea." There are still a few old-fashioned tea shops around, but the best bet for a family is to go to Fortnum and Mason's. This is much more that a grocery store, although that's how it started. The Royal Family gets its food there. (Don't expect to find the Queen pushing her cart down the frozen food aisle, however.) Their restaurant offers tea for very good value each afternoon for about £7. Dress, less formal here than at some places, is "smart casual." You'll be offered a choice of teas, and can choose from a selection of dainty sandwiches and wonderful pastries. You will leave utterly stuffed and feeling so veddy-veddy English.

Do the English still take tea? Go to that cricket match to find out. They actually interrupt the match at about 4:30 for a little while so the players can have their cakes and cuppa.

Remember, not everybody has to do the same things at the same time on this trip. If the genteel sports fans want to go to the cricket

Tea—and High Tea

match while the genteel (but hungrier) sports cynics want to take tea, everybody's happy. Meet back at the flat later to compare notes. And the cricket fans needn't go hungry. Concession stands do sell some ballpark-like fare such as sausages and beer, but you can also dine on smoked salmon sandwiches and vintage wine. Civilized.

Recommendations

✔ Spend a half day just romping and relaxing in the park. A Sunday picnic at Hyde Park during warm months is ideal.

✔ Find a small local park or square near your lodgings where you can relax in the evening and chat with local residents.

✔ Do something stereotypically English like attending a football or cricket match or taking afternoon tea.

15. Shopping and Street Markets

W hat's the last thing your kids probably want to do when they're on vacation? The answer may vary from family to family, but we'd bet in many cases, it would be: *Shop!* Well, maybe. Shopping is a chore for most kids, except when they're looking at things *they're* interested in. That seldom happens when they're dragged along on adult shopping excursions. Since this is a family trip, though, we're going to talk about a few places the younger family members might enjoy browsing.

We recommended in Chapter 7 that you give each child a certain amount of spending money. Once you do, it becomes theirs, and it's probably best not to exercise too much control over how they spend it. What looks like a pointless bit of junk to you could be the most memorable souvenir a child brings home.

The best way to make sure they don't get burdened with real junk, though, usually is to avoid the glitzy souvenir shops that spring up near every tourist attraction. You'll know what we mean when you see them near Parliament or St. Paul's. They all sell the same refrigerator magnets and plastic models of Big Ben. Stop in one if you want. There are a few cute things (usually overpriced) and some inexpensive things (usually junk) there. But no more than one: they're all the same. Except for one item—tee-shirts—there are better pickings elsewhere, both for buying and for just window shopping.

Kids come in all ages and interests, so trying to list where to buy everything is an impossible task: the Central London Yellow Pages has 1,840 pages of small type. We'll point out some of the best places to go for the kind of shopping most kids might be interested in, but you'll find other places you like as well.

Toys

If you want to see your younger kids wide-eyed, we've got two places that will make them hyperventilate. It's like being transported to Santa's workshop just before he packs the sleigh. A few paragraphs don't do justice to these places: youngsters from four to 84 can spend a whole day entranced by toys, dolls, and games of every description.

When shopping, consider how you'll pack for the trip home

If your kids want to buy toys at the same store that Prince William (Charles and Diana's oldest son; he'll be the king in about 30 years) and other royal children get theirs, **Hamleys** is the place.

Hamleys holds a royal warrant, which means that it is an official supplier of goods to the Royal Family. The store is on Regent Street not far north of Piccadilly Circus. There may be no better place in the world to buy a teddy bear, a toy car, a doll, or a train than Hamleys.

Unless it's **Harrods**. At what is probably the most famous department store in the world you can buy a box of pins or you can outfit a jungle expedition—or anything in between. The toy department is on a huge scale, like everything else in Harrods. You may find enormous

---

A Shrine to Food

While you're at Harrods, don't miss the Food Halls. Just a quick walk through will give you an appetite you'll never satisfy. We could happily wander room to room, up and down aisles, for hours wondering just who eats (or who can afford!) such gastronomic wonders.

Our favorite departments for gawking are the cheese section, extensive enough to awe even a Wisconsin dairy farmer; the candy department, too delicious and wonderful to bear contemplation from thousands of miles away; and, for an exhibit of almost museum quality, the seafood counters. Even people who don't care for fish will enjoy the artful presentation of more varieties of fish than you'll see in an aquarium.

Even if Harrods were nothing but a grocery store, its food halls would be worth a tube ride down and an hour's sightseeing. With so many other fascinating and unique departments available, it's on nearly every serious shopper's "must do" list.

---

sculptures of Lego bricks, model train layouts snaking around like a plate of spaghetti, dolls and doll houses enough to populate a fair-sized doll city. Harrods is on Brompton Road just south of Hyde Park *(Tube: Knightsbridge on the Piccadilly line)*. Pick up a free guidebook for the store from one of the racks inside each entrance. A brief warning: Harrods tries to project an image of class. Shoppers that its doormen consider inappropriately dressed— men in shorts, people wearing tee-shirts with offensive sayings, and so on—may be refused admission to the store.

Music

If you're looking for records, tapes, or CDs, we've already given you a lead on the best places: **Tower Records** at Piccadilly Circus (there are other locations but this is the best), the **Virgin Records Megastore** at 14–16 Oxford Street near Marble Arch, and **HMV Records** at 150 Oxford Street. These are three cavernous music stores. You'll also find smaller shops in the Soho or Covent Garden areas that specialize in used records or collectors' items, but avoid buying new tapes from the vendors you'll see on the streets. They're selling pirated copies, for the most part, and the quality can be poor. What's more, U.S. Customs inspectors can confiscate pirated tapes when you get back to the United States.

Books and Comics

What a daunting category! There are too many to choose from! But we must, so we'll send you to our favorite bookstore, **Dillon's**, for new books. The best branch is the one at 82 Gower Street, WC1, about two blocks north of the British Museum. They have everything, but their travel section is truly wonderful. Be careful, though. You'll often find the same book, at widely differing prices, in separate sections. If you're shopping along Piccadilly, go to **Hatchard's** for books at No. 187. It has as many followers as Dillon's and is just as well stocked. In addition, there are countless specialty bookstores throughout London.

For books of *any* sort, but especially for second-hand books, wise shoppers will walk up Charing Cross Road. There are dozens of stores there, some general and some highly specialized. You could spend the day in **Foyles** at 119 Charing Cross Road if there weren't so many other enticing places. The bibliophile in your family may wish to go no farther than Charing Cross Road, but if you go to MOMI, check out the second-hand book market underneath Waterloo Bridge near the South Bank arts complex. The books there range from popular fiction to classics to 300-year-old collectables. You can eat an inexpensive lunch at the National Film

Theatre Restaurant next to the book market and there are always buskers nearby to entertain you as you eat and browse.

There are good second-hand bookshops in the streets near the British Museum, too, but these are more often rare or collectors items and prices are higher here.

Readers of fantasy or science fiction should look into **Forbidden Planet** at 71 New Oxford Street, near Tottenham Court Road. They also stock a wide selection of role-playing game materials. For comic book readers or collectors the choice is **Gosh Comics** across the street from and half a block west of the British Museum. They also have a good array of cartoon books based on British comic strips. Or try **Comic Showcase** at 76 Neal Street in Covent Garden.

Posters and Local Souvenirs

There are many places to buy posters, but the easy choice is the gift shop of the **London Transport Museum** in Covent Garden. If you're looking for a poster that has anything to do with London, there's not even a second best to consider. The place with the nicest and the widest variety of London-related items is the gift shop at the **Museum of London**. Of all the gift and souvenir shops in all the tourist attractions in London, we rate these two the best. But if they enjoyed the museum, kids will certainly want to stop in the gift shop at the **Museum of the Moving Image** for television and movie souvenirs.

Tee-Shirts and Other Clothes

This is one time that stopping at one of those kitschy souvenir shops might not be a bad idea; their tee-shirt inventory is excellent. Our favorite design is the shirt imprinted with the map of the Underground system.

But someone is bound to want a tee-shirt from the **Hard Rock Cafe**. You'll find the restaurant at 150 Old Park Lane, W1. The street runs north off Piccadilly at a tangle of streets across from Green Park near Hyde Park Corner.

Some things should never be taken as souvenirs!

Want to take home some funky threads? You'll find plenty to choose from just walking up and down the streets in Soho, but since the 60s the shops of **Carnaby Street** (oddly, it's just a bit east of the very stuffy shops of Regent Street) have been magnets for the young and hip. You can also find all sorts of fun-to-wear clothes at the **Portobello Road Market** described below.

Window Shopping and General Browsing

If you want to look at expensive goodies but not buy them, **Harrods** is fun. The **Burlington Arcade** on Piccadilly is a covered arcade with some of London's classiest and most expensive shopping. On the South Bank a good choice for browsing is the **Hays Galleria** near London Bridge. The architecture of this tony shopping mall is impressive and it has a nice selection of stores that travel book authors can't afford to shop in. The same could be said of the many interesting and elegant shops in the neighborhoods surrounding Harrods. This area of South Kensington is a window shopper's paradise, although that might not be the kids' idea of a great time.

More reasonably-priced goods may be found up and down **Ox-ford Street**. Perpetually jammed with shoppers, you'll find the first-rate **Selfridge's** department store, **Marks & Spencer**, and scores of other general-interest and specialty shops on this street. Christopher Place, a quiet little street of interesting boutiques and quaint shops, runs north off Oxford Street.

Scottish woollens are available throughout the city, but some of the best prices and selection are available at **Westaway and Westaway**, across the street from the British Museum. And if you have your heart set on fine china from Wedgewood or Royal Dalton, you can find good bargains at the **Reject China Shop**. There are branches all over London and their stock changes constantly, but they usually carry seconds of some of the best-known china, some with flaws you just can't find, for a fraction of what you'd pay in a department store.

Street Markets

For a taste of London that's miles removed from the dignity of Harrods and the British Museum, shop at one of London's many markets. Easiest is **Covent Garden**. It's central, easy to get to, well supplied with food and entertainment, and lots of fun. Depending on the day of the week you'll find crafts, antiques, or general merchandise featured, and there are good bargains if you keep your eyes open. But London has many other markets. Another good market for crafts and handmade furniture is **Gabriel's Wharf**, just east of the South Bank arts complex along the Thames.

There are smaller neighborhood markets like the one on Church Street near Regent's Park. This one attracts no tourists, just the local residents who come here to buy food, housewares, and clothes. Some are like the one on Warwick Way in Pimlico, that specialize in fruits and vegetables and other foodstuffs for the people who live in the area. These are places to see the ordinary people of London living lives uncomplicated by tourists, and if you're staying at a flat near a market like these, that's where you should shop, too, if you're really trying to live like a local.

But a fun outing for everyone is to one of the big markets. **Camden Market** *(Tube: Camden Town on the Northern line)* is open

Shopping and Street Markets

Saturdays and Sundays and has a terrific array of hip clothing and music. **Petticoat Lane** (*Tube: Aldgate—Circle line; Aldgate East—Metropolitan line*) is open on Sundays and specializes in housewares and clothes, although scores of vendors offer almost anything else you can think of. Unfortunately, on our last visit we saw far too many instances of drug sales and use here.

Best bet for the whole family, we think, is the **Portobello Road Market** (*Tube: Notting Hill Gate—Circle, District, and Central lines*) on Saturdays. This is a crowded and exciting series of streets with hundreds of stalls and shops where you can buy ancient Roman coins for a couple of pounds, fine jewelry for thousands of pounds, cool clothes, old records, rare books, signs and posters, sports equipment, electronics—pretty much anything you can think of.

It's easy to get separated here so be sure you establish a meeting time and place. The kids, if they're old enough, will enjoy browsing on their own more than they will with you anyway. A word of caution: keep track of your wallet or purse here. Pickpockets do work the crowds at markets. Oh, yes: Don't be too quick to pay the price quoted; almost all the vendors expect to bargain. If you offer a lower price than the one marked, you'll probably get a better deal.

We have just a word of advice in conclusion. The possibilities for shopping in London are so great that it's easy to let it get out of hand. Come armed with two things: a limit on how much money you're willing to spend shopping, and a list of the people you're buying souvenirs for. Shopping here is fun, but mementos need not be expensive. A hand-dipped candle from an ancient castle or a 300-year-old clay pipe found in the Thames might cost only two or three pounds but be a more fitting souvenir than a £150 Wedgewood vase. The best souvenirs are usually the ones that bring back the nicest memories, not the ones you paid the most for. This is a good time for your children to learn that.

16. Walking Around London: On, Off, and Around the Beaten Track

L ondon, as noted previously, is a compact place, and this means that it's pretty easy to get from place to place on foot. And there are certainly many things in London best enjoyed on foot (we'll get to some of those later in the chapter). But sometimes, if you plan on walking from Site A to Site B, getting there can be half the fun—or more.

First, though, a caution. If you walk *anywhere*, and you have very young children, it's best to keep it short—a few blocks, maybe from one neighborhood to another—unless you can carry them or are willing to put up with the whining ("whingeing" on London's side of the sea). Mike recalls that his own childhood family walks around the neighborhood always concluded with a chorus of piping voices complaining "I'm hungry and thirsty and tired!" (Sorry about that, Mom and Dad.) Remember, though, children half your size will feel like they are walking twice as far or more. Give them a break—if you're not sure, you can always take the tube.

Walking Around London

Walking, even walking aimlessly, is really the *best* way to get acquainted with London. Walks can be a family event, or the teenagers may want to break out for a while on their own, or you can split into groups, or maybe *you* just feel like walking. We've assumed that you've already read Chapter 6 for information on walking around safely. Chapter 6 will also give you basic information about walking around London and things like maps, which you will need if you follow the advice we're about to give you.

Our advice is: *get lost!* No, we're not being rude—we don't mean for you to put the book down and scram. Neither do we mean to literally lose your way and become stranded in London somewhere. (If this *could* happen, though, you'll be prepared after you read the sidebar "If You Get Lost" in this chapter.) No, what we mean is a great way to spend an afternoon is to pick a place on your map that looks interesting and just go there. Or, consider walking home from the museum or monument you're planning to visit instead of taking the tube. We guarantee that you'll find interesting things on the way, things you would have missed if you had taken the tube.

If you decide to take a walk, make sure you have your map. But *don't* stick to the streets on the map; use it to orient yourself instead. It's a good idea to know at least vaguely where you are and about where the nearest tube station is. You may find a secluded neighborhood park. Or an interesting monument the guidebooks don't mention. Or a fascinating place of worship. Or a shopping mall. Or a restaurant you'd love to try. Or maybe a residential area—imagine what it would be like to live there. There's no better way to shake hands with London than to walk its streets!

Some areas of London, of course, are more interesting than

If You Get Lost

You suddenly realize that nothing looks familiar, you can't remember how you got to where you are, and the map is a jumble. You are really lost. What now?

---

others. Many people don't find the business and banking areas of the City particularly fascinating, for instance. One of the authors thinks the most interesting thing about it is all the people in their identical suits scurrying down the streets at certain times of the day. ("People watching" can be fun too.) The other author has found urban character in narrow old streets and crusty Victorian buildings tucked away behind boring concrete office blocks—but admittedly not much for kids. The beauty of London is that if you come to a dull spot you can simply walk right past it! If worst comes to worst, you can pick another area to hang around and catch the tube.

The possibilities are endless. We have a few ideas to get you started, but the places you will

---

1. Don't panic. *As silly as it may sound, your heart may pound, you may start to sweat, and you may have the urge to run, yell, or do something drastic. Just let it pass and try to calm yourself. You're really not in any danger; you're just disoriented.*

2. Ask for help. *You will not seem foolish if you ask a passerby or store clerk for directions. Everyone, even Londoners themselves, gets lost sometimes, and Londoners are generally very helpful. Instead of asking how to get back to your flat or hotel (unless it's nearby), you may instead want to ask how to get to a street or landmark that you think is close by, from where you can get your bearings. Or, ask where the nearest tube station is. A surprising number of London residents carry maps themselves whenever they venture out of their neighborhoods.*

3. If all else fails, *retrace your steps. Keep your map handy. Eventually you will come upon a street or intersection that you can find on the map.*

IF YOUR CHILD IS LOST: Make sure your child knows what to do if he or she gets lost. Police officers are easy to find, or can be delivered up immediately by calling the national emergency telephone number of 999 from any phone. If small children are lost, that's what they should do, call a police officer and wait in a safe public place with supervision, like a shop or even a pub. Older kids ought to be able to follow the tips above and find themselves again.

There's one more good emergency measure for the hopelessly lost: hail a taxi and tell the driver

London has many open public squares

most remember are the ones you discover for yourself. It seems hard at first to justify coming all this way just to wander around without spending all your time at famous tourist attractions. But *where you want to go. He knows where everything is. But take heart: Nobody ever gets lost for good in London. We've been lost many times and enjoyed it! London is easy even for young teens to navigate. Carry your passport, your local address and phone number, and a map, and you'll never have a problem.*

a quiet afternoon strolling through a neighborhood *without* those crowded attractions will usually produce some memorable discoveries. Here, then, are a few of *our* favorite areas for walking.

Along the Thames

We find that a walk along the great River Thames, on *either* bank, is always interesting, and the further you walk, the more you see, both the typical tourist sights like Parliament and Tower Bridge, and less typical attractions like the large art-deco Battersea Power Station.

London for Families

You can start from anywhere along the river, but a good choice is Wesminster Bridge, near Parliament. As you walk east from there along the north side of the river, you're walking along the **Victoria Embankment**. The walkway here was built in the 1860s to control flooding, and runs alongside a busy street. It doesn't take long to forget the noise and traffic fumes, though, because your attention is quickly focused on the river and on the interesting collection of buildings on the other side. Most striking is the one at the other end of Westminster Bridge, the old London County Council Hall. It has been just a collection of offices since the council was disbanded in 1986, but there are plans to turn in into the sort of luxury hotel we've counseled you to avoid. But you can always look at it for free!

Walk along the north side of the river, enjoying the view, until you come to the third bridge, Blackfriars Bridge. There's an interesting and historic pub here, the Black Friar (named for the dark robes of the monks whose monastery was located here centuries ago), which has some of the most appealing pub decor in England.

Waterskiing on the Thames is a bad idea

Cross the bridge to the South side of the river and head back along the **South Bank**. This is one of London's most delightful walks. There's no noisy street nearby, it's less crowded, there's plenty of room for the kids to run off some energy, and the architecture across the river is fascinating. Near the South Bank Arts Center you'll find a large plaque that will help you identify all the buildings on the other side. You can stroll all the way back to your starting point or beyond, along the Albert Embankment, clear to Battersea Park, though that would be a pretty long hike.

We seldom take this entire walk at once, but we find ourselves drawn to the river often during our visits, and cover both sides of the Thames, between the Westminster and Brackfriars bridges, in stages during every visit. It's an ideal energy restorative.

> ***Tip:*** *The walk along the South Bank at night is one of London's greatest visual treats. The walkways are illuminated, as are the dramatic buildings along the way. If the tide is out there are steps down to the riverbank where you can enjoy even more peace and solitude in the midst of a city of millions.*

To the Palace

On our walk in Chapter 6 we took you to Buckingham Palace through Green Park. Another appealing walk in that direction starts at Trafalgar Square. At the southwest corner of the square stands Admiralty Arch—you can't miss it. Go through the Arch and you're on one of the broadest and most picturesque streets in London, **The Mall**. Buckingham Palace is an easy fifteen-minute stroll (or a determined eight-minute walk) straight ahead. St. James's Park runs along the left side of the Mall, and as you approach "Buck House," St. James's Palace is on your right. The Mall is a perfect thoroughfare for a queen riding in a horse-drawn carriage. You probably won't get to see that, but the Mall makes it easy to imagine.

Canal Walks

Regent's Canal runs across the entire north side of London and provides plenty of opportunities for a peaceful walk. You can start from Regent's Park near the Zoo and walk for miles along the waterway, through Camden Town, Islington, and Bethnal Green.

The attraction for us in walking along the canal is that it cuts through so many everyday, non-tourist areas of London—the sort of places we'd probably live if we lived in the city. After all the history and glitter of the famous buildings and museums, we enjoy the reminder that, after all, most people are pretty much like us . . . and that's a good thing for your kids to keep in mind, too—people are just people, whoever and wherever they are. It's a joy to walk for a while, then to find a neighborhood park to relax, play, or chat in before resuming our stroll.

Note that at Islington the canal goes through a tunnel for several blocks while the footpath continues above ground on city streets; they're well marked and will take you back to where the canal resurfaces.

Where Else?

If you've read this far in the book you've already discovered plenty of other places to try. Consider what you need:

- Somewhere for the kids to run around and play? Any park will do, or perhaps Coram's Fields just a few blocks east of the Russell Square tube station. It's a large park with playground equipment, but adults are admitted only if accompanied by children.
- A place to wind down after a busy day? Find a place with water—the river, the canal, the Serpentine.
- Bright lights and people-watching opportunities? Piccadilly Circus, Chinatown, or Soho at night are perfect.

Approach London just as you do your own home; begin with the neighborhood you live in and get to know it, then branch out. There are interesting places everywhere, and you'll miss them if you spend all your time whizzing past them in a taxi or zipping under them on the tube. London *must* be walked to be appreciated for all that it is.

Recommendations

✔ Explore your neighborhood thoroughly. Wherever you live, it's a microcosm of the city as a whole. Not everything has to be historic or opulent.

✔ London at night from the South Bank: Don't miss it.

✔ Take care of your feet because you *should* do a lot of walking. Put bandaids on sore spots at once, wear two pairs of socks if you need to in order to prevent blisters. But don't let sore feet slow you down.

17. Daytrips

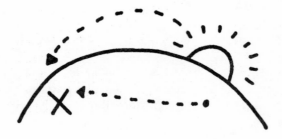

We've spent sixteen chapters telling you what marvellous things your family can do in London. So why are we encouraging you to get out of town in this chapter? Because England is so rich in history and beauty that it ought to be a punishable offense not to take advantage of some of the *other* wonderful things the island has to offer.

We urge you to take one out-of-town trip for every week of your holiday. In this chapter we suggest a dozen destinations. All are less than two hours from London and it's possible to see the highlights of each, at least, in a single day. Each destination is accessible by train because, while it's easy to rent a car in England, train travel is so relaxed and convenient that only people with more obscure destinations in mind will find a car more useful.

Train Basics

British Rail (the natives never say "Britrail" even though it's marketed abroad that way) was recently privatized, and the railway system now consists of numerous companies serving different routes and sections of the country. On short routes some of the rolling stock is aging and may be quite warm in the summer, but its longer routes are served by comfortable air-conditioned coaches. It's a lovely way to travel and one-day trips are not expensive.

If you're going out and back on the same day, always ask for a "cheap day return" ticket. Its cost will be just nominally higher than a one-way fare, whereas a regular return ticket (not "round-trip") may be double the one-way fare.

If you plan on doing a lot of travelling, Britrail passes are available from any U.S. travel agent. They are *not* available in Britain. A good bet is the "Flexipass," which is good for four days of travel in an eight-day period, or for eight days, or fifteen days in a month. They're much cheaper than an unlimited pass and good value unless you're planning to travel almost every day.

We don't recommend buying first class tickets. They're much more expensive than second, or standard, class, but carry no real advantages for a family. Standard class is clean and comfortable and seats are much roomier than airline seats. In every case we're aware of, the standard class cars arrive at the station just as quickly as the first class cars they're connected to—the ones with a yellow stripe painted above the windows. Save your money.

Trains almost always leave on time—to the second. Be on board! Also remember that you cannot buy tickets on the train as you often can elsewhere. If you board without a ticket you may be charged the highest fare on that route plus a substantial penalty. One more thing worth remembering: London has many railway stations. Make sure you know which one your train leaves from! The listings below will name the destination, the railway station at your destination, the approximate number of trains per day, the distance, and the average travel time, and information about the railway station. We'll describe the highlights of each place very briefly, but each could use an entire chapter to do it justice. You can always pick up a local map, often free of charge, and other information about local attractions, in or near any railway station.

Travelling at 100 miles an hour across the lovely English country-side, looking out big picture windows while on your way to a fascinating city: this is one of the things we look forward to. Let's go!

Bath

More than 20 trains a day from Paddington Station; 107 miles, 1 hour 25 minutes. The station is on Manvers Street, a ten-minute walk south of the principal attractions.

Bath repeatedly wins competitions as Britain's cleanest, or friendliest, or most beautiful city. It has everything you could want: ancient Roman ruins, a fine medieval church, spectacular architecture, eye-popping scenery.

The Romans built a grand health spa here and a tour of the Roman baths is an absolute must. The museum here contains enough wonderful Roman artifacts and sculptures to delight anyone in your family who has ever been intrigued by the Roman Empire. Stop in the Pump Room near the entry to the Baths for a famous Bath bun and a drink of the mineral-laden water that bubbles up from the spring. Bath Abbey was founded in the 7th century, and the present church was begun in 1499. The overlook in front of the church across the River Avon offers a stunning view of hundreds of buildings of the distinctive reddish-cream "Bath stone" which is the area's chief architectural characteristic. The view is especially beautiful in late afternoon.

Spend an hour or two just walking around this gorgeous city and if you can, take a late train back to London so you can sample the quiet beauty that envelopes it, even at the height of the tourist season, after all the tour buses have gone home.

Brighton

More than 30 trains a day from Victoria Station; 51 miles, 1 hour. The station is a 15-minute walk north on Queens Road from the beach.

Brighton is where Londoners go on a day outing to the seaside. There is a long broad beach where the hardy splash in the cold Channel water and where everyone else sunbathes. Be aware that

You'll probably want to wear shoes at Brighton Beach

like most beaches in Europe, tops are optional for women here and perhaps one in ten choose to go topless. Americans notice, but no one else gives it a second thought.

While sunbathers have to decide whether to wear the upper halves of their swimsuits, another part of the clothing ensemble is less open to question. Wear shoes or sandals on the beach! There's no sand here, but rather miles of little round stones. The barefoot bather unused to stone beaches will walk slowly and uncomfortably along the waterfront and probably flee to the esplanade behind the beach at the first opportunity.

Palace Pier, which stretches out a quarter-mile into the English Channel, will attract kids like a magnet. In its center is a large old-fashioned penny arcade, although games for a mere penny disappeared long ago. But £5 will buy a child a lot of fun for an hour or so. Brighton has many other museums and attractions; even the walk along Queens Road to the beach is pure glitz. But don't miss at least walking past the Royal Pavilion, a gaudy, fanciful home in mock Indian style built for King George IV in the 1780s before he came to the throne.

Cambridge

More than 30 trains a day from King's Cross Station; 56 miles, 1 hour. The station is about 1½ miles from the city center. The no. 1 bus will take you from the station to St. Andrew's Street in the heart of town for about 50p. You can catch the bus back to the station when it's time to leave. It's impossible to go astray doing this.

Cambridge is, of course, one of England's two great seats of learning. Cambridge University is actually a collection of more than two dozen largely independent colleges, each with its own history, tradition, and governing body. You're welcome to wander in and out of many of them, sometimes for free, sometimes for a small fee of £1 or less, which may also get you a small pamphlet or printed tour. There are so many things to see here that a list is hard to compile, but don't miss the Gothic splendor of King's College Chapel, showplace of the entire university. The gates into many of the colleges, some of which date back more than 600 years, seem to compete with each other for ostentatiousness, and are in stark contrast to the lush, quiet greens that lie behind them.

When you're tired of walking, you can hire a punt (a small boat propelled by pushing a pole along the river bottom) and go punting on the River Cam. There are always Cambridge students eager to make some extra money by driving your punt and giving you a witty tour of "The Backs," the river area that runs behind many of the colleges.

College tee-shirts being popular among kids from every country, expect yours to have no difficulty in finding a Cambridge University shirt to buy.

Canterbury

More than 20 trains a day from Victoria Station; 62 miles, 1 hour 40 minutes. Check with the conductor to make sure you're on the right car: the train sometimes divides en route. Canterbury East station is a 15-minute walk from the Cathedral across the footbridge and along the city wall.

Pilgrims old and new go to Canterbury

While the station is a fifteen-minute walk from the cathedral, the walk is part of the attraction. Cross the footbridge that goes over the highway and you'll find the ruins of a 900-year-old Norman fortress. Continue along the old city wall around the modern business area, keeping the towers of the cathedral in sight—you can't miss it.

The cathedral itself is one of the grandest in England. When you see too many great medieval cathedrals, they tend to run together in your mind, but this is one that stands out. Now a simple candle marks the spot where St. Thomas Becket was martyred by soldiers of his friend King Henry II. This was once one of the great pilgrimage destinations in Europe, as you recall from Chaucer's *Canterbury Tales*.

Canterbury offers blocks of quaint streets and centuries-old buildings in the area north of the cathedral, and is famous for its teddy bears. "Canterbury Bears" are famous among collectors throughout the world and there are several stores along the old streets. Look for *Teddy's Emporium* at 50 Northgate for a special souvenir for someone fond of stuffed animals.

The ruins of St. Augustine's Abbey, among the earliest Christian sites in England, lie a block east of the city walls. Founded in the 7th century, the old abbey is the burial site of some early Saxon kings.

Greenwich

Just seven miles from Central London, Greenwich can be reached by Docklands Light Railway, which leaves from the Cannon Street or Tower Hill Underground stations. A train is available from Charing Cross Station for the 12-minute trip. The best way to go, however, is by boat. The 30- to 45-minute trip, depending on the tide, leaves from Westminster pier at least every 30 minutes.

Our closest daytrip is only minutes from London proper, but Greenwich (pronounced *Gren*-itch) is like stepping into another part of the world. You'll find little traffic, few lines, and no noise in this peaceful suburb. There are attractions enough that even if you spend a whole day here, you'll want to come back for more. We'll limit ourselves, though, to the things that are most likely to capture your kids' attention.

Don't be afraid of Greenwich Mean Time

Stroll through Greenwich Park, one of the Royal Parks, and huff and puff your way up the hill to the Old Greenwich Observatory. This was once the world's most important spot because the basis for our measures of time and geography were set here. The Prime Meridian—zero degrees longitude—passes through here, and practically every tourist poses for a picture straddling the line . . . one foot in the Western Hemisphere and one in the Eastern. This is also the home of Greenwich Mean Time, the time from which all others are measured.

The Royal Naval College is located in Greenwich and provides fascinating glimpses of the past and present of the naval force that won the world's most far-flung empire. The Queen's House, home of the wife of the unlucky Charles I (the king who lost his head in 1648 during the Civil War) is another grand palace whose opulence helps visitors understand why contenders for the throne used to kill each other off with distressing frequency. Who *wouldn't* want to live in such elegance?

Closer to the river, the kids will enjoy scrambling around the *Cutty Sark*, last of the great India clipper ships. Visitors have access to almost the entire ship and there's a memorable collection of old wooden mastheads belowdecks. You can get a combination ticket that permits access to the Observatory, the *Cutty Sark*, and several other attractions, or you can pay for each individually. You can have a full day for less than £10 each in admissions.

Hampton Court Palace

Two trains per hour from Waterloo Station make the trip in 30 minutes; a boat from Westminster Pier takes two to three hours depending on the tide, and offers a scenic, relaxed morning trip up or afternoon trip home again. The boat docks at the Palace; the railway station is a few hundred yards from the entrance on the other side of a bridge over the river.

Who is not fascinated by Henry VIII? This was his favorite residence, a sprawling palace built by his one-time friend Cardinal Wolsey, who wisely gave it to the king when Henry admired it and "suggested" to the Cardinal that it would make a fine gift. Built around three courtyards, the palace oozes history. Be sure to take the audio tour of the *royal kitchens*. Unlike most audio tours, it's free and provides a captivating peek at the preparation for a

16th-century royal banquet. There's also an audio tour available of the "new" part of the palace built in the early 1700s, but it costs and some members of the family might not have the patience for two such tours. If that's the case, a quick walkthrough of the *state apartments* will give a good taste of the opulence of the place.

Then go outside and enjoy the gardens. Highlight is the famous maze, sure to be fun for everybody. The object is to get from the entrance to the center, then back out again. It's tricky, with dozens of blind alleys and switchbacks, but tell everyone if they get hopelessly lost that there's a secret to it. The maze is one continuous hedge, so just follow it. Keep the hedge always on your right hand side and turn every time it does. You'll cover every part of the maze that way but you'll never get lost. It's the "short cuts" that take extra time.

You can wander the grounds for hours, enjoying the gardens, the 200-year-old grape vine, the world's oldest (or perhaps second oldest, depending on who you believe) tennis court, the art gallery, and much more. It's a full day.

Leeds Castle

Near Maidstone, Kent; about 40 miles from Central London. At Victoria Station ask for a special ticket that includes admission to the castle. Leave the train at Maidstone to board a special bus operated by British Rail that will take you the remaining 15 minutes to Leeds Castle. The bus returns at least hourly from the drop-off point.

Leeds Castle may really be what its publicity claims: the most beautiful castle in England. It sits in the middle of a lake surrounded by lush parkland, a true fairy tale setting; it really *looks* the way we think of a castle looking, with drum towers and crenelated walls. It's another site associated with Henry VIII. He probably met Anne Boleyn here. She lived not far away, at Hever Castle, and was probably a lady-in-waiting for Henry's first queen, Catherine, when she visited here. But Henry was only one of the castle's royal owners. It dates to more than 300 years before his time and at least thirteen kings have held this building beginning with Edward I in 1297.

Parts of the inside of the castle have been modernized, because Leeds was a private home between 1552 and 1974, when it was turned over to a preservation organization. But there are many period rooms which echo the building's long history as you tour it. There is much to see on the grounds, too. Children may be interested in seeing one of England's strangest museums, the Dog Collar Museum, and there is another excellent maze. Get to the middle of the maze and you're at the entrance of an underground grotto that will delight all ages with its fanciful stonework.

Oxford

More than 30 trains a day from Paddington Station; 64 miles, 55 minutes. The station is on the west side of town while most of the colleges are east, but the walk is a pleasant 15 minutes through the city center along Hythe Bridge Street and George Street; it's not possible to get lost.

While there's little in Cambridge that's not associated with the university, Oxford is a larger, more industrial city. But cross the shopping district into the precincts of one of the world's oldest universities, and you're again surrounded by green space and serenity. The best way to see the colleges is to join a tour leaving from the Information Centre on Queen Street. Led by Oxford students or sometimes retired teachers, they'll show you nooks and crannies you'd have trouble finding on your own, and take you into some of the colleges closed to the casual visitor. Cost of a tour is £4–5.

More British political leaders and literary figures are associated with Oxford than with anywhere else. If any of your children enjoyed *The Hobbit* or *The Lord of the Rings* books, J. R. R. Tolkien was a student at Exeter College and a professor at Merton College. C. S. Lewis, who wrote *The Narnia Chronicles*, was also a student and professor here. Near Merton College is one of England's oldest pubs, the Turf, which was more than a century old when the first colleges were founded in the mid-1200s.

For a breathtaking view of Oxford, "The City of Spires," as it calls itself, pay a pound to climb the tower of St. Mary's Church. The vista is unforgettable. The claustrophobic should stay on the ground, however, because the ancient steps are twisting, steep, and very narrow.

Stonehenge and Salisbury

Nearly 20 trains a day from Waterloo Station to Salisbury; 84 miles, 1¹/₂ hours. The station is in the northwest part of town. A bus can be taken from the station directly to Stonehenge for about £4 round-trip. To see the Cathedral, keep your eyes on the spire, the tallest in England, and stroll through Queen Elizabeth Gardens to the church.

The 4,000-year-old mysteries of Stonehenge remain unsolved. No one knows for sure who built it (it wasn't druids, who came here a thousand years too late) or why, but seeing this towering, silent monument on the gently rolling plain is fodder for your imagination. The site can be busy during the summer months, which does dampen the mystique, and it's no longer possible to go right up to the stones. They've roped them off because too many people were scratching their initials in them and chipping off little souvenir pieces. The closest approach is now about fifteen yards. Thirty minutes to an hour is sufficient for seeing the site, and the bus will take you back to the railway station.

The grand Salisbury Cathedral is worth the trip in itself. Built in the mid-1200s it has some of the most beautiful stonework in England. As you approach the church, note that its spire, rather like a famous tower in Italy, leans noticeably. The spire was added after the church was built and the foundation wasn't adequate to support it properly. The support columns inside the cathedral are slightly bowed from the weight of the 400-foot-high tower. But it's stood for more than 700 years so there's no immediate danger of its giving way.

There also are interesting ruins about two miles north of Salisbury, at the original site of the town, Old Sarum, which was abandoned in the early 13th century. You can get a city bus from the bus station near the Guildhall.

Stratford-upon-Avon

Trains go from Paddington Station to Leamington Spa, where you change trains to Stratford. Trains are also available from Euston Station to Coventry, where you are met by a "Shakespeare Connection" bus which goes to Stratford. Six to ten trains a day. The total 120-mile trip takes 2 to 2$\frac{1}{2}$ hours. The bus station is at the north side of town, close to the historic attractions; the railway station is a ten-minute walk west of the city center.

The birthplace of William Shakespeare is an attractive Midlands town that holds some of England's most revered literary associations. The 16th-century house in which he was born is certainly authentic and worth a visit, although the bed in which he was supposedly born is of more dubious origin. His burial place, Holy Trinity Church, is at the south end of this small town. The town is a pleasant one to walk through, past locations connected with the great poet. The most attractive place, however, is Anne Hathaway's Cottage, in the tiny village of Shottery, best reached by a footpath. It's a pleasant fifteen-minute walk and ends near her cheery thatched cottage, which is surrounded by a lovely garden.

Children may enjoy watching boats on the canal that winds through Stratford. There are locks in the park which raise and lower the boats, and watching the process makes for an interesting and relaxing half-hour.

Stratford is one of England's prime tourist destinations and consequently is usually crowded. The feel of a small English village is difficult to capture among the queues and souvenir shops, but this is a "must" pilgrimage for those who revere the work of England's most influential literary figure.

Warwick Castle

About six trains a day from Paddington Station to Leamington Spa, where a bus or taxi is available for the two-mile trip to the castle. 110 miles, 2 hours.

If you were an invader and caught sight of this fortress in the distance, you'd turn around and go home muttering to yourself. Stand atop Guy's Tower, the great drum tower, and you have an utterly impregnable feeling. This castle, above all others in England, gives you the sense of what a medieval castle was like. The grounds and buildings are open, and there is an excellent display, created by Madam Tussaud's, called "The King Maker," about the early knights and battles for the throne. Another exhibit shows castle life in the more genteel days of a late 19th-century house party.

The *armoury* is one of the best collections of old weapons you'll see, and the *dungeon* is far superior to the one you'll be shown if you stand in line at the Tower of London.

It's quite possible to see Stratford and Warwick on the same trip. It makes a full day but you get a taste of two very different sides of English history.

Windsor Castle

Three trains an hour from Waterloo Station; 25 miles, 50 minutes. The station is a short walk through the city center from the castle.

Windsor Castle differs from the others in this chapter because it is still a royal residence. The Queen comes here often, and when she is in residence her standard flies above the great Round Tower. Windsor is the largest working royal castle in the world and, because of its proximity to London, its population is swelled with legions of tourists. The crowds shouldn't dampen your good time, however, because there's much to see.

Centerpiece of the castle is *St. George's Chapel*, opulent home to another of the great orders of chivalry, the Knights of the Garter.

Minstrels may greet your arrival at Warwick Castle

The chapel was completed by Henry VIII in 1528. He is one of ten monarchs to be buried here. Others include Charles II, first king after the English Civil War, and George III, who presided over the American Revolution.

The tour of the *state apartments* is as eye appealing as that at Hampton Court, but with a distressing difference. A terrible fire destroyed a large section of the apartments in November 1992, and restoration work will continue for several years. Much of it is being paid for by admissions to the Buckingham Palace tours each summer.

We hope you'll find an out-of-town trip that appeals to everyone, but don't be afraid to split up, with some family members going to one destination and the rest to another, then comparing notes at the end of the day. The chance to see a little of the countryside or some of the stately palaces or picturesque cities of England is an experience that should not be missed.

Part III:
Planning Pages

I n Part I we tried to suggest the things you needed to know to book your trip and the survival skills your family would need in London. Part II focused on what to do when you got there by reviewing many of the best known, and some lesser-known, London attractions and highlighting what we thought were the best places for *families*.

In this section we'll try to simplify your planning. First, we'll review the attractions we've talked about and put them in a form for your family to check off their favorites. Next we will suggest a number of mix-and-match itineraries you can use as a basis for planning your sightseeing on trips of varying lengths. Finally, we will give you a simple form for projecting your costs so you can get down to the business of booking your trip!

18. Top Attractions

I n the first seventeen chapters we talked about more than 100 places to go and things to do. How can you take such a large amount of information and make some sense of it? That's what we'll try to help with in this chapter.

Listed below are all the things we've talked about, together with the chapter number where we dealt with each in some detail. We've already suggested that everyone in your family read at least the chapters in Part II, and that you've talked together about what you might be interested in doing. If a vacation like this is going to be as exciting and memorable for everyone as you want it to be, *everyone* should be involved.

Now we'd like to suggest that you make one photocopy of the attractions list in this chapter for each member of the family. Agree on a plan for people to choose the things they like the best, and tally up the results. Now you have the makings of your family's itinerary.

The first time *our* family did this we asked each person to take the list and mark each item as something they were

- *strongly interested* in seeing or doing
- *somewhat interested* in

- *neutral* about
- *not interested* in seeing or doing, or
- *did not want* to see or do

We also asked each person to list his or her top three things that they wouldn't want to miss, no matter what. Then we tallied the votes and ranked the attractions. That gave us a rough order of priority of things to see and do, but we made two exceptions.

First, we gave more weight to the kids' votes. The trip was intended to be for them, and for all of us as a family, and we wanted to make sure that they got to do as much as possible of what interested them. Larry and Barb knew they'd have other chances to go by themselves and follow their *own* interests, but our days of travelling as a whole family were numbered. (Ulterior motive: Kids who are doing what they've voted to do are probably going to be more pleasant and agreeable than those who have to spend time at things they think are boring.)

Second, we made sure that *every* person got his or her top choice, even if nobody else voted for it. We all agreed in advance to be flexible, cheerful, and tolerant of the things that were important to the others in return for everyone else being tolerant of each of us.

Once we had the list of what we *wanted* to do, we began working out itineraries to see what was *possible* to do. That involved some juggling, but we held true to our commitment to get everybody's first choice on the final list.

This might be a more complicated approach than your family needs, and that's OK. It's *your* vacation, after all! What's important is that everyone takes part in the planning process, and that everybody gets to see the things they *really* want to see.

Every family is different, of course, but we've also highlighted in bold type the things *we* believe are "don't miss" attractions for *any* family.

Here's the list:

MUSEUMS

- ☐ Bethnal Green Museum of Childhood [Chapter 10]
- ☐ **British Museum and Library** [10]
- ☐ Cabinet War Rooms [10]
- ☐ Dickens' House [10]
- ☐ Globe Theatre [10]
- ☐ Guinness World of Records [10]
- ☐ HMS Belfast [10]
- ☐ Imperial War Museum [10]
- ☐ London Dungeon [10]
- ☐ London Toy and Model Museum [10]
- ☐ London Transport Museum [10]
- ☐ Madam Tussaud's [10]
- ☐ Museum of London [10]
- ☐ **Museum of the Moving Image (MOMI)** [10]
- ☐ Natural History Museum [10]
- ☐ Pollock's Toy Museum [10]
- ☐ Science Museum [10]
- ☐ Sherlock Holmes Museum [10]
- ☐ Victoria & Albert Museum [10]

HISTORY AND PAGEANTRY

- ☐ Banqueting House [11]
- ☐ Blue Plaques hunting [11]
- ☐ **Ceremony of the Keys at the Tower** [11]
- ☐ **Changing of the Guard** [11]
- ☐ Fleet Street [11]
- ☐ Inns of Court [11]
- ☐ Livery Companies Exhibition (July) [11]
- ☐ Royal Tournament (August) [11]
- ☐ Shakespeare Country [11]
- ☐ St. Martin-in-the-Fields Church [11]
- ☐ Temple Bar area [11]
- ☐ **Tower of London** [11]
- ☐ Trooping the Color (June) [11]

MUSIC, THEATRE, ART

- ☐ Abbey Road [12]
- ☐ Bayswater Road artists [12]
- ☐ **Buskers** [12]
- ☐ Courtauld Institute [12]
- ☐ Globe Theatre [10, 11]
- ☐ Hyde Park Concerts [12]
- ☐ **National Gallery** [12]
- ☐ National Portrait Gallery [12]
- ☐ Rock Circus [12]
- ☐ Tate Gallery [12]
- ☐ **Theatre: Go to a play** [12]
    - ☐ Theatre: Fringe [12]
    - ☐ Theatre: Little Angel Theatre [12]
    - ☐ Theatre: Open Air [12]
    - ☐ Theatre: Polka Children's Theatre [12]
    - ☐ Theatre: Unicorn Theatre for Children [12]
    - ☐ Theatre: West End [12]

CHURCHES, BRIDGES, AND OTHER GRAND STRUCTURES

- ☐ Buckingham Palace [13]
- ☐ Kensington Palace [13]
- ☐ The Monument [13]
- ☐ **Parliament buildings and Big Ben** [13]
- ☐ Parliament debates [13]
- ☐ Roman Wall [13]
- ☐ St. Bride's Church [13]
- ☐ St. James's Palace [13]
- ☐ **St. Paul's Cathedral** [13]
- ☐ Temple Church [13]
- ☐ **Tower Bridge** [13]
- ☐ **Westminster Abbey** [13]
- ☐ **Westminster Bridge** [13]
- ☐ Westminster Cathedral [13]

PARKS AND DIVERSIONS

- [ ] Cricket [14]
- [ ] Cruises: Canal and Thames [6]
- [ ] Green Park [14]
- [ ] Hampstead Heath [14]
- [ ] Highgate Cemetery [14]
- [ ] **Hyde Park** [14]
- [ ] Kensington Gardens [14]
- [ ] London Zoo [10]
- [ ] Picnicking in the Royal Parks [14]
- [ ] Regent's Park [14]
- [ ] **Speakers Corner (Sundays)** [14]
- [ ] St. James's Park [14]
- [ ] Tea [14]
- [ ] Tower Bridge Park [14]

SHOPPING AND STREET MARKETS

- [ ] Books: Charing Cross Road, Dillon's, Hatchard's, Waterloo Bridge [15]
- [ ] Burlington Arcade [15]
- [ ] Clothing: Westaway and Westaway, Selfridge's, Marks & Spencer [15]
- [ ] Comics and Fantasy: Gosh Comics, Forbidden Planet [15]
- [ ] Hamley's [15]
- [ ] Hard Rock Cafe [15]
- [ ] Harrods [15]
- [ ] Hay's Galleria [15]
- [ ] London Transport Museum gift shop [15]
- [ ] Markets: Covent Garden [15]
- [ ] Markets: Gabriel's Wharf [15]
- [ ] Markets: Portobello Road, Camden, Petticoat Lane [15]
- [ ] Markets: small, local shopping [15]
- [ ] Museum of London gift shop [15]
- [ ] Oxford Street [15]

Top Attractions

- Record Stores: HMV, Tower, Virgin Records [15]
- South Kensington shopping [15, 19]
- Souvenir shops for tee-shirts [15]

WALKING IN LONDON

- Albert Embankment [16]
- Chinatown [6, 19]
- Coram's Fields [16]
- **Covent Garden** [6]
- Guildhall [11]
- **Lains' Guided Walking Tour of Central London** [6]
- **The Mall** [16]
- **Neighborhood Walks** [4, 16]
- **Piccadilly Circus** [6, 16]
- Regent's Canal [16]
- Soho [16]
- **South Bank of the Thames** [16]
- Southwark [11]
- **Thames Walk at night** [16]
- **Trafalgar Square** [6]
- **Victoria Embankment** [16]
- **Whitehall and No. 10 Downing Street** [6]

DAYTRIPS

(We haven't highlighted anything here, although Hampton Court is probably our favorite nearby destination and Bath and Canterbury our favorite longer trips. None of these places will disappoint, however.)

- Bath [17]
- Brighton [17]
- Cambridge [17]
- Canterbury [17]
- Greenwich [17]
- Hampton Court Palace [17]

☐ Leeds Castle [17]
☐ Oxford [17]
☐ Stonehenge and Salisbury [17]
☐ Stratford-upon-Avon [17]
☐ Warwick Castle [17]
☐ Windsor Castle [17]

OTHER THINGS TO SEE AND DO

☐ Bus ride on top a red double-decker
☐ Canal cruise
☐ River cruise

☐ _____
☐ _____
☐ _____
☐ _____
☐ _____
☐ _____
☐ _____
☐ _____
☐ _____
☐ _____
☐ _____
☐ _____
☐ _____
☐ _____
☐ _____
☐ _____
☐ _____
☐ _____
☐ _____
☐ _____
☐ _____
☐ _____
☐ _____

19. Sample Itineraries

E very family is different, and only by going through the planning process can the members of *your* family decide what's
right for *them*. But in this chapter we will present some
sample itineraries, not to set your schedule for you, but to show you
how it is possible to put together days that are varied and well paced.

The key is to remain flexible. If you have outdoor activities
scheduled, like a morning at a street market and an afternoon at a
cricket match but get torrential rains instead, choose a day full of
indoor activities. But don't be *too* quick to change all your plans.
While we've almost always had wonderful weather on our trips to
Britain, we've had plenty of fun in the rain, too, even on outdoor
walks. It's a matter of attitude.

In our sample itineraries, we normally don't specify a day of the
week, except where certain events are limited to specific days.
Otherwise, days are interchangeable depending on the weather,
your mood, and the interests of your family. Take out anything that
doesn't appeal to you and add anything we don't include that you'd
rather do. We try to put together a number of options for each day,
and to select things that are either clustered together or are easy to
travel between.

Admit in advance that you can't possibly do everything. London is too large and varied for that. We've been there many times and haven't even *begun* to see and do everything we're interested in. That's not so bad, though: It just gives us an excuse to go back again! By the way, don't forget to watch for Blue Plaques whenever you're out walking, and remember to watch for special events and festivals.

One-Week Itinerary

Arrival Day—This might be any day of the week, but if you've followed our advice for inexpensive travel, you left home on a Monday through Thursday, and so will arrive on a Tuesday through Friday. Follow the advice we gave you in Chapter 4 about spending *your first six hours in London*. You've moved in, taken a short nap, explored your neighborhood, had a good meal, and shopped for groceries, snacks, magazines and newspapers, and bought your tube passes. By now it is probably 3 p.m. and many of the museums and attractions will be closing in a couple of hours. If you're living near one that you especially want to see, go now and spend 90 minutes or so. You won't be happy unless you begin seeing what you came for, but remember our caution not to overdo it your first day. So what *we* suggest is a short walk that will show you a few of the famous sites.

Take the tube to the Westminster Underground station, cross Westminster Bridge, and take a relaxed *walk along the South Bank* of the Thames. Or stay on the north side of the river and *stroll along the Victoria Embankment*. Either way, you'll get a good view of Parliament and Big Ben, and if you're up to it you can walk all the way down to Blackfriars, which is something over a mile downriver, where you can see the dome of St. Paul's. For a shorter walk, stop and take the tube back from the Embankment or Temple Underground stations north of the river or Waterloo on the south side. Make a fairly early night of it tonight. The next few days will be busy and your body craves sleep. Get to bed by 10 o'clock and you'll be completely adjusted by morning.

Sample Itineraries

Day 2—We're up early, have fixed breakfast in our flat or polished off the spread our hotel provided, and are ready to do some serious sightseeing. Now is the time for the *Lains' Walking Tour* described in detail in Chapter 6. Take this at your own pace and feel free to stop off along the way to visit some of the attractions you pass. It's easy to get waylaid by the Changing of the Guard, at Westminster Abbey, or in Covent Garden! If you don't finish the walk today, you can always pick up later where you left off.

You can stop for a light pub lunch along the way, but if you don't get delayed *too* long by irresistible attractions on the walk, you ought to get to *Covent Garden* about lunchtime. That's perfect because there are dozens of places to eat around the market. You can find baked potatoes the size of footballs, crepes with dozens of types of fillings, hamburgers and fries, ethnic food of every description, all within a block of the center of the market. Spend at least an hour here eating, watching the people and the buskers, perhaps shopping. The London Transport Museum, and for the thespians in your family, the Theatre Museum, are here, too.

By the time the walk takes you to Leicester Square, you may be ready for an ice cream cone at the shop on the north side of the park. If you'd like to plan an evening at the theatre tonight, check the board outside the *half-price ticket booth* and make a list of shows to see. Then one person can stand in the queue to buy tickets while the others see the attractions in the area. *Chinatown, Trafalgar Square*, and the *National Gallery* are all within a five-minute walk of the ticket booth. Decide on a time and place to meet, and when you're finished, take the tube home again. Rest for a while before supper, fix a simple meal in the flat or eat at a nearby restaurant, then set out for your *evening at the theatre*. If going to a play isn't your cup of tea, spend the evening in the park reviewing the day or making plans for tomorrow while your feet rest.

Day 3—Lots of options today but we'd definitely begin at the *Tower of London*. Get there early and see the Crown Jewels, take the tour, and spend an hour or two seeing some of the many other attractions. You can get a simple and inexpensive lunch at the cafe there and shop, if you're inclined, in the large gift shop. When you're finished at the Tower, you have several choices. You can't go wrong.

• Just east of the Tower Hill tube station is a bus stop. A no. 15 bus stops here every ten minutes or so. Board the westbound bus (same side of the street as the Tower) and take it to *St. Paul's Cathedral*. The ride through the City is interesting, especially from the top of the bus, and you can't miss your stop . . . *or*

• When you leave the Tower, walk along busy Byward Street Hill, which runs along the north side of the Tower. Turn right at the corner and walk across the famous *Tower Bridge*. You can stop in the middle and take a memorable photo of the Tower itself, and once across you'll get a spectacular view of the bridge. From here you can walk along the river to our walk through *Shakespeare Country*. Also nearby are the *London Dungeon* and *Hay's Galleria*. If Shakespeare isn't what you're after today, you can catch the no. 501 bus eastbound from London Bridge or Southwark Cathedral and take it to the South Bank arts complex and spend the rest of your afternoon at the *Museum of the Moving Image*.

After supper tonight, find a place for an evening walk if the weather is good—perhaps down *The Mall* or through one of the *Royal Parks* or *Inns of Court*. If you've made arrangements in advance, this would be a good night to view the *Ceremony of the Keys* at the Tower.

Day 4—If you were out late last night after the Keys, sleep late today. After breakfast go to Buckingham Palace for the *Changing of the Guard*. Be there by at least 11 a.m. to get a good place to watch. The ceremony runs from 11:30 to 12:30.

• Your next destination might be historic *Westminster Abbey*. It's an easy walk from the Palace down Birdcage Walk or through St. James's Park to George Street and Parliament Square. You should have no trouble finding an inexpensive lunch at a sandwich shop or pub near either the palace or the abbey.

If you spend two hours in the abbey, you can have an interesting finish to your afternoon by walking a block to the river. Westminster Pier is at the foot of the bridge, and is an ideal place to take a *river cruise*. You can take a tour boat that will take you a ways upriver and down, along with anecdotes and running commentary, lasting an hour or so, or for much less money you can just board the river taxi for a 15- or 20-minute run down to the Tower. You'll get less description from the captain but will still see the wonderful views and, with the help of your map, you can easily pick out the most important landmarks for yourself. At the Tower, you can catch the tube home again. If you prefer, you can leave the boat at the Swan Lake Pier at London Bridge (check when you buy your ticket to make sure your boat will stop there) and walk up a block to climb the *Monument*. You can get

---

Rainy Days

What happens if it rains? Well, to begin with, always carry an umbrella. Rain will seldom be more than a minor nuisance as you go from place to place. Most days on our itineraries include both indoor and outdoor activities. If the weather is inclement, just substitute something else for today's outdoor event.

Most of the time you shouldn't let a little rain slow you down, although a monsoon may require a different strategy. A walk along the river in the rain can be as pleasant as at any other time. A light drizzle will keep some people away from the Changing of the Guard, making it easier for you to find a spot where you can see well. A picnic, it's true, isn't much fun in the rain, and the cricket match is apt to be postponed, but otherwise life goes on pretty much as normal. Rain will ruin your day only if you let it.

If forecasts call for a very inclement day, visit the museums of South Kensington: Science, Natural History/Geological, Victoria & Albert. They're all very much worth going to and you can go from one to another via underground tunnels. If you get tired of the museums, hop aboard a no. 14, 74, or C1 bus for a dry five-minute trip to Harrods.

Or, you could all just hop on a double-decker bus and see where it takes you—then find your way back on the tube. The Tower, Westminster Abbey, and the British Museum can literally occupy a full day each if you want, and will make you forget the rain.

continued on page 238

a tube home from there, too. . . . or

• If you visited St. Paul's yesterday and have had your fill of grand churches, you could go to the *London Zoo* instead. From Buckingham Palace, walk through Green Park and enter the Underground station that's on your right when you get to Pic-

> *Rain in London seldom lasts all day; it is much more likely to be showery than rainy, with dry periods throughout the day. Since you'll probably do much of your travelling underground, the rain may not be much of a bother. But if you've bought this book, rather than just borrowed it, we grant to you the luck of the Lains: The weather we've had in London has never failed to be beautiful. We've never had more than two rainy days on any trip, even trips for as long as five weeks. Our assurance is no guarantee, but it's the best we can do.*

cadilly. Take a northbound train on the Jubilee line to Baker Street: that's just two stops. From Baker Street you can catch a no. 274 bus that will take you to within a short walk of the zoo, or you can walk east on Marylebone Road, past *Madam Tussaud's* and turn left at the corner into Regent's Park, and walk through the park to the zoo, about 20 minutes altogether.

• Remember that splitting up may be a good choice sometimes. This might be a good afternoon for older kids to pick something they would like to do that the rest of the family isn't interested in. You can meet at home later to compare notes.

Back at the flat tonight, just relax, watch some TV or read the papers, and write your postcards. You've had several busy days and should recharge your batteries with a quiet evening.

Day 5—If you're leaving day after tomorrow, don't forget to call your airline this morning to reconfirm your reservations.

London is wonderful, but so are some other places. We have our choice of some nearby places where we can have a fun outing without wasting any more travel time than necessary. For a short excursion, we recommend either *Hampton Court Palace* or *Greenwich*.

The train trip to Hampton Court is just a half-hour train ride from Waterloo, while you can get a train from Charing Cross to

Sample Itineraries

Greenwich that takes just twelve minutes. The Docklands Light Railway line from near the Tower is even faster, if that's more convenient.

Go first thing in the morning and spend as much of the day as you like. There are enough varied things to do to keep you busy all day, but if you want to come back to London in mid-afternoon to work in an extra museum, pick up some theatre tickets, or see another attraction on your list, both daytrips are close enough to make that easy.

Tonight you can take in another play if you're a theatre-going family, perhaps a fringe show. Maybe there will be a concert worth going to. A walk in a part of town you won't otherwise get to see is a nice way to spend an evening. But our choice might be to go back down to the river at dusk and see the spectacular sights of the *Thames at night* when the Houses of Parliament, Big Ben, St. Paul's, the Tower, Tower Bridge, and everything else is brilliantly spotlighted. A late supper at a riverside pub like the Anchor Bankside will provide a grand view of the City. Cross the river at London Bridge and take the tube to Embankment or Westminster and go back to the South Bank and you'll have a view that will give you chills and spectacular photos. (A fast film of at least ISO 1000 will give the best results.)

Stay up late tonight and gaze at the sights, if you like. Tomorrow will be your last full day in town.

Day 6—There is still too much to do! We'll just have to come back another time. There are great museums to see and shopping to do. Let's get on with it! You might choose one of these museum-shopping packages:

● Start at the *British Museum and Library*. There's plenty there to keep you occupied for hours, but limit it to just two. Afterwards, get a bite to eat at one of the many inexpensive restaurants near the museum. (There are also some very expensive ones, so check the menus outside.) There are books and comics and woollens to buy within a hundred yards of the museum entrance, but when you finish there, turn left on Bloomsbury Street (the street that runs on the west side of the museum) and go up to New Oxford Street. Turn right on New Oxford Street for a mile and a half of London's busiest shopping area. . . . *or*

• Start at the *Science Museum* or *Natural History Museum* or *Victoria & Albert Museum* in the South Kensington area. Any of these (but especially the Science Museum) will fascinate and educate everyone in the family. When you've had all the museum you want, turn left up Cromwell Road. Just past the V&A the street becomes Brompton Road, a mecca for serious shoppers. The street is lined with a cornucopia of stores, the centerpiece of which, a half-mile up the street, is Harrods, a tourist attraction in itself.

When you've finished today's museum and shopping excursions, you have every reason to treat yourselves to dinner at a nice restaurant. This is your last night in London, after all. Take a last walk around your neighborhood, and do your packing. What a great trip!

Departure Day—There will be little chance to do sightseeing today. Most flights to North America depart between 11 a.m. and 2 p.m. to arrive in time for passengers to catch connecting flights home. This will be a day that's at least 29 hours long, because you'll regain the hours you lost on the flight over. Retrace the procedure you took to get from the airport to your lodgings in Chapter 4, giving yourself plenty of time. Most airlines recommend getting to the airport at least two hours before an international flight. Soon you'll be homeward bound with pictures, memories, and a special family bond that wasn't there before.

Two-Week Itinerary

A longer stay gives you the chance to spread out some of the key sights. If you stay for *one* week you might have to decide between Westminster Abbey and St. Paul's, or between the British Museum and the Science Museum. With a longer stay you can do both. In this section, we will show you how 14 days *might* work, but what you include, and how you mix-and-match your activities depends

Sample Itineraries

on what interests *your* family, not the Lains! We do suggest varying your activities each day. We often suggest evening activities, but if your children are young, you should stick close to their regular bedtimes and you'll spend more evenings at home. In any case, we think that evenings in your flat or hotel are necessary every few days just to catch your breath. Watch TV, play a game—whatever you normally do at home.

Day 1—As in the One-Week Itinerary

Day 2—As in the One-Week Itinerary

Day 3—The *Tower of London* as above. Then take the bus to *St. Paul's Cathedral*. When you finish at St. Paul's, spend a half-hour wandering around the area, then home. Tonight attend the *Ceremony of the Keys* while the Tower is still fresh in your mind.

Day 4—*Changing of the Guard, Westminster Abbey, river cruise,* and a quiet evening at home.

Day 5—Take a daytrip today. Since we have more time, we don't need to limit ourselves to Hampton Court or Greenwich, although they're surely worthwhile. Any of the destinations in Chapter 17 will do nicely. If you're not too tired when you get back, and if the weather is good, the night walk along the Thames is still a good idea. Be sure to fit it in before you leave.

Day 6—The *British Museum,* and shopping along Oxford Street today. Instead of shopping, the kids might like to head to Piccadilly Circus to see Rock Circus, the Guinness World of Records, and to shop at Tower Records. If people want to go out tonight, walking around colorful Chinatown and crowded Soho can be fun.

Day 7—Start the day at the *Museum of the Moving Image*. If the afternoon is fair see about attending a *cricket* or *football* match. If your cricket match is at the south London stadium called the Oval, you can spend some time at the *Imperial War Museum*. People who aren't sports fans might browse the shops along Piccadilly (or go to Rock Circus or the Guinness World of Records), window shop the *Burlington Arcade*, and go to *tea* at Fortnum and Mason. An alternative afternoon might be to take one of the numerous and inexpensive guided walks. Brochures describing them are everywhere and they're listed in *Time Out*. Relax at home tonight.

Day 8—Today is a day for the young and young at heart. Start at the *Bethnal Green Museum of Childhood*. From there, take the tube two stops west to Bank Street and change to the Northern line. The third stop north is Angel, near the *Little Angel Marionette Theatre*. Finish the day by taking the tube one more stop north to King's Cross and changing to the Piccadilly line. Go south to Piccadilly Circus, where you're a short walk from *Hamley's toy shop*. If your kids are too old and sophisticated for a day like this, they're probably old enough to spend at least half the day on their own, away from parents, seeing the sights *they* want. *Planet Hollywood* and the *Hard Rock Cafe* are close to each other in the Piccadilly Circus area, and are close to *Covent Garden*, which is ideal for kids to hunt for souvenirs and to just hang out at. Tonight you'll probably need to go to the store and stock up again, or will need to do some laundry.

Day 9—The *Science and/or Natural History Museum* today, followed by shopping in South Kensington and a visit to *Harrods*. Tonight: Check your bus map and climb aboard a red double-decker to spend an hour riding and gawking in a direction you haven't seen yet. If possible go back by bus on a different route or take the tube.

Day 10—If you haven't spent a *day in the park*, you should. If you don't feel like the park today, walk up *The Strand and Fleet Street*, have lunch at *Ye Olde Cheshire Cheese*, then walk north from St. Paul's to the *Museum of London*. Visit the museum or look for *Roman ruins along London Wall*. Tonight you might like to go to the theatre again. A West End show is fine, but also check out the *fringe shows* for a cheaper, and perhaps very different, alternative.

Sample Itineraries

Day 11—Choose a destination for a *daytrip* out of town. If you can't agree on one, split up, but nobody should travel alone: It's *much* more fun with a companion. Relax at home tonight and finish your postcards, even though you'll get back before they will.

Day 12—Reconfirm your flight reservations today. Start the day with *Tower Bridge, Tower Bridge Park, and Shakespeare Country.* If you have the energy, walk along the river to Waterloo, stopping at *Gabriel's Wharf* to sightsee and shop. Or cross the river at London Bridge and climb the *Monument.* Relax by taking the tube from Waterloo to Charing Cross or from Monument to Embankment, then strolling over to *Trafalgar Square* to spend some time people-watching. For a little culture, visit the nearby *National Gallery* or *National Portrait Gallery.* Tonight, begin to get organized for your trip home. Make sure you've finished your shopping and seen the sights you're most interested in.

Day 13—Spend today in the *Regent's Park* area. Take a *canal trip,* go to the *Zoo,* visit *Madam Tussaud's* or the *Planetarium,* stop at the *Church Street Market* for a glimpse of a neighborhood shopping market. If it's a nice summer day you couldn't do better than to have a picnic supper in the *Rose Garden* and attend a performance at the *Open Air Theatre.* Finish your packing tonight.

Saturday Option—To experience the fun of a big street market, begin your day at the *Portobello Road Market.* Even the kids will probably take at least three hours to get bored with this. After lunch from one of the street vendors, choose afternoon activities from the suggestions above.

Sunday Option—We've said more than once that a lovely summer Sunday can be found by taking a pile of newspapers and a picnic lunch to *Hyde Park.* Listen to the speakers at *Speakers' Corner.* Read, eat, talk, play, relax, and revel in your family being together in this place. Remember to stroll along the *Serpentine* and to check out the artists along *Bayswater Road.*

London for Families

Departure Day—As in the One-Week Itinerary

Three-Week Itinerary

By this time we've gone through many of the places of general interest. During a three-week trip you will have a chance to visit some of the sights listed among the first two weeks above that you skipped, and places which may have less broad appeal but in which you have special interest. We've talked about a number of those in earlier chapters. For a *three*-week trip, though, we think you'd want to consider adding some of the following activities:

● At least one more daytrip, or perhaps a two- or three-day trip, with a stay at a B&B, to somewhere like York (two hours away by train), Wales (Cardiff, the capital, is two hours away), Edinburgh (four hours), or Penzance (five hours).

● If your only visit to the museums of South Kensington has been to the Science Museum, do visit the Natural History Museum or Victoria & Albert Museum. Both are stuffed full of wonderful and surprising things.

● Kensington Palace. Admission to *this* royal palace costs less than half the tariff of the house of the reigning Queen, and has much to gawk at.

● More days in the park. We especially like Hampstead Heath, where you can ramble through both woods and fields, and from which (atop Parliament Hill) there is a spectacular view of London. There's no better place in London for the kids to enjoy the outdoors.

● Specialty sights and museums for those with particular interests. Possibilities include such things as the Old Operating Theatre Museum, the Sherlock Holmes Museum, attending a session of Parliament, the Cabinet War Rooms, the Clink, the Unicorn Theatre for Children, and so much more.

Sample Itineraries

- A visit to London's principal place of worship for your faith.

However long you stay, London will surprise and delight you daily if you give it a chance. Dr. Samuel Johnson, 18th-century London sage and the man who compiled the first important dictionary of the English language, once said, *"When a man is tired of London, he is tired of life; for there is in London all that life can afford."* What was true in Johnson's day is no less true in ours. The problem in preparing an itinerary for a vacation in London is not in deciding what to include, but in deciding what must, however reluctantly, be left out.

20. Planning and Budget Worksheets

Planning and organization are the keys to a successful and economical vacation, whether you're visiting your state capital or going abroad. We've talked about all the things you ought to know, about scores of attractions you might visit. In the previous two chapters we've talked about how you can organize your sightseeing on your family trip. In this chapter we'll offer a short but useful guide to organizing your travel and budget plans. We'll follow the outline we provided back in Chapter 1, and provide forms you can use to prepare for your trip.

Planning and Budget Worksheets

Form I: Your Flight

This is information your travel agent will need to find your best rate.

1. **How many people travelling?** _____
   _____ Adults   _____ Children under 18 (ages: _____)
   _____ How many students?
   Depending on the route and the time of year, discounts may be available to students or children under a certain age.

2. **Departure date:** _____
   Is this date ☐ **fixed** or is it ☐ **flexible?**
   If you can travel during low or shoulder season, airfares may be half or less of high season (summer months) fares. Avoid Friday, Saturday, and Sunday departures. If you can be flexible, your agent may be able to find better rates.

3. **Length of stay?** _____ days/weeks
   Stays of 7 to 30 days usually qualify for the cheapest rates. Avoid return flights on Friday, Saturday, and Sunday for better rates. Remember that a flight originating in the U.S. usually arrives in Europe the next day, so if you leave home on June 1 for seven days, schedule your accommodations for the nights of June 2–8 with a return flight on June 9.

4. **Preferred airline, if any?** _____
   If you or another family member works for an airline, you may be eligible for deep discounts. Do you have a frequent flier account with an airline? If so, foreign travel can add considerable mileage. Do you have enough miles in an account to get one or more tickets free? Do you want to start an account with a particular airline?

5. **Preferred airport, if any?** _____
   You might save money by driving to a more distant airport where cheaper fares are offered. Ask your agent to price flights from all nearby airports.

6. **Non-stop flight required or connection OK?**
   ☐ Non-stop only; ☐ connection OK
   Unless you live near a city with non-stop service, this isn't an issue: you'll have to connect. But if there's a choice, the connection might be cheaper. If you have a choice of connecting cities, consider scheduling your flights to give yourself time for an excursion into the most interesting city. Make sure easy public transportation is available from the airport to city center.

7. **Stopover en route OK?**
   ☐ Yes; ☐ No
   A few foreign carriers offer deep discounts to travellers willing to stay overnight in their countries, but accommodations and extra meals can eat away savings on airfare.

Armed with this information, you and your travel agent should be able to help you find the very best fares available. Don't stop watching for sales after you buy your tickets, either. Airlines will often reissue more expensive tickets at sale prices for a service charge.

Enter your airline fare in the appropriate place on Form III.

Planning and Budget Worksheets

Form II: Accommodations

This is what you need to consider in booking your lodgings

Do you want a hotel or a flat? We think a flat is better for a stay of a week or more, but you must judge your own family's needs. The table below offers some very realistic comparisons.

Cost *per Person/per Night* for Various Accommodations
based on a value of £1 = $1.60

	3 PEOPLE IN FAMILY	4 PEOPLE IN FAMILY	5 PEOPLE IN FAMILY
HOTEL @ £150 PER NIGHT	$80.00	$60.00	$48.00
HOTEL @ £100 PER NIGHT	$53.33	$40.00	$32.00
HOTEL @ £60 PER NIGHT	$32.00	$24.00	$19.20
FLAT @ £750 PER WEEK	$57.15	$42.85	$34.29
FLAT @ £500 PER WEEK	$39.10	$28.57	$22.86
FLAT @ £350 PER WEEK	$26.67	$20.00	$16.00

For purposes of comparison, a night at a Holiday Inn or similar American chain, at a rate of $75 per night, would cost $25 per person/per night for three people, $18.75 for four people, and $15 for five people.

To find comfortable lodgings, decide whether you wish to stay in a hotel or to rent an appartment, and use one of the forms below—

IIa for hotels and IIb for flats. Make a short list of attractive-sounding accommodations from the information gleaned from the London Tourist Board book and other sources described in Chapter 2. Spot their locations on your map. Then telephone the manager of each hotel or estate agent for each flat on your list and ask questions like those below. This will allow you to confirm the information in the book, to get a feel for how knowledgeable and helpful the manager is, and to negotiate the price.

Complete a form like those below for each lodging you consider, then sit down and make your decision. Booking several months ahead, particularly if you're going during the summer, is a good idea.

IIa. Hotel Questions

- I'm looking for a room for _____ people for these dates: _____

- Is the room *en suite*? (i.e. with a toilet and tub or shower)

- If the room has a shared bath, how many rooms share it?

- If the room is *en suite*, how much can we save with a shared bathroom? If it has a shared bathroom, how much extra would it cost for room *en suite*?

- Describe the room:
  How many beds (single and double)?
    Are cots available for extra children and at what price? (*Request a discount for bringing a sleeping bag or your own bed linens for the cot.*)
  What other furniture is in the room? How large is it? (*A drawback to hotels is that single rooms can be uncomfortably snug . . . and they get smaller the longer you stay!*)
  Can we get two connecting or adjoining rooms? At what price? (*Ask if you can get one room with toilet and one without to save a little extra.*)

Planning and Budget Worksheets

- Do rooms have televisions and telephones?

- Do you have rooms with cooking facilities?

- Is a full English breakfast provided? If yes, describe it. When is it served?

- Do you have lifts?
  (*That means elevators. We don't care very much if he puts something in his shoes to appear taller.*)

- Where is the hotel located? Describe the neighborhood. Is the area residential, commercial, industrial? What kinds of restaurants are nearby?

- How far away is the nearest . . .
  . . . Underground station?
  . . . bus stop?
  . . . park or public square?
  . . . self-service laundry?
  . . . grocery store?
  . . . local street market?

- Do you accept credit cards? Traveller's cheques? Do you require a deposit?

- What is the best rate you can give me? Does it include VAT?

After asking questions like these of several hotel managers, you should have all the ammunition you need to get a comfortable, convenient, and economical hotel.

Multiply the rate per night by the number of nights you will stay, and enter the total in the appropriate place on Form III.

IIb. Apartment Questions

- I'm looking for a flat for _____ people for these dates: _____

- Describe the flat:

  How many rooms does the flat have?

  How many does it sleep?

  How many beds (single and double) and where are they located?

  Is there a sleeper sofa which can accommodate some people?

  Are cots available for extra children and at what price? (*Request a discount for bringing a sleeping bag or your own bed linens for the cot.*)

  How is the living room furnished? Sofa, chairs, lighting, other furniture.

  How large is it? Is there television and telephone?

  What kind of storage do the bedrooms have? Closets, dressers, etc.

  How is the kitchen equipped? Cooking utensils, plates, glasses, cups, silverware, stove, refrigerator, electric kettle, storage space, hot water, pots and pans, etc.

  Describe dining facilities? Is there a separate dining room or a dining table in the kitchen or living room?

  Does the bathroom have a tub or a shower?

- Are bed linens and towels provided? Cleaning or maid service?

- If the flat is upstairs, is there a lift?

- Do you have laundry facilities for guests?

- Where is the flat located? Describe the neighborhood. Is the area residential, commercial, industrial? What kinds of restaurants are nearby?

Planning and Budget Worksheets

- How far away is the nearest . . .
  . . . Underground station?
  . . . bus stop?
  . . . park or public square?
  . . . self-service laundry?
  . . . grocery store?
  . . . local street market?

- Do you accept credit cards? Traveller's cheques? Do you require a deposit?

- What is the best rate you can give me? Does it include VAT?

- Is your rate per day or per week? If weekly, must I rent for complete weeks or are additional days chargeable on a *pro rata* basis?

After asking questions like these of the managers or agents for several flats, you should have all the ammunition you need to get a comfortable, convenient, and economical apartment.

Enter the total rent in the appropriate place on Form III.

Form III: The Budget

This will give you a reasonable estimate of your total expenses

Dollar amounts are calculated at £1 = $1.60. Keep an eye on the exchange rate; if it changes, adjust the conversion factor below. For example, if the exchange rate changes to £1 = $1.55, multiply the amount in pounds by 1.55. If it changes to £1 = $1.70, the multiplication factor is 1.7.

1. **Airfare costs** $ _____
   from Form I

2. **Lodging**   _____ £ _____ × 1.6 = $ _____
   from Form II

3. **Food: meals and snacks**
   • *If you're staying in a hotel, you'll probably eat two meals per day—lunch and dinner—in restaurants. If that's the case, allow £12 to £15 per person/per day for meals, depending on the ages of your children.*
   • *If you're renting a flat and plan to fix breakfast and supper at home most of the time, eating only lunch in restaurants, figure £8 to £10 per person/per day, a figure which also takes the purchase of groceries into account. It's possible to spend much more, of course, but these figures will provide comfortably.*

   Per person/per day £_____
     x number of days   _____ = £_____ × 1.6 = $_____

4. **Attractions and sightseeing**
   There are many free attractions. Even adding a West End play each week should keep the figure well under £10 per person/per day. We'd figure no more than £6 or £7 per person/per day.
   £6 x _____ people x _____ days = £_____ × 1.6 = $_____

5. **Shopping and souvenirs**
   This is a very personal category. We suggest you give each

Planning and Budget Worksheets

child a fixed amount, perhaps $25 to $50, or a sum of
perhaps $5 to $10 per day to pay for souvenirs, snacks, etc.
They can, of course, supplement that with their own money
if they wish. Mom and Dad can set their own budget in this
category. However, we do recommend that you set a fixed
amount in advance. Give the money to your children in
pounds when you arrive, perhaps a little at a time for
younger ones. $_____

6. **Local transportation**
   - A tube pass will cost about £12 per person/per week
     £12 × number of people
     × _____ weeks   =   £_____

   - Airport transportation:
     from Heathrow, the Airbus cost is
     about £5 per person each way
     £10 × number of people =   £_____
              or
     from Gatwick, the Gatwick Express
     is about £8 per person each way
     £16 × number of people =   £_____

   - Taxi from Airbus stop or Victoria at
     beginning and end of trip should
     be £8 or less per trip   =   £ 16

   - Daytrips. Short trips to Hampton Court,
     Greenwich, or Windsor may cost
     less than £5 per person. Longer
     excursions from Chapter 17 may
     cost up to £25 per person = £_____

   Total   £_____ × 1.6 = $_____

Total Expenses in Categories 1 through 6 above $_____

To be on the safe side we usually add a contingency fund of
about 10% of the total. We've never needed it, but it's nice to have
a cushion.

Glossary

It's good to have as few surprises as possible when communicating with locals anywhere, and England has many words and usages that differ from usual American speech. Here are a few of the most common "Britishisms," followed by their definitions in American English. You'll undoubtedly discover more! In fact, sharing the new words and phrases members of your family have heard each day makes fun dinnertime conversation.

bangers and mash: sausages and mashed potatoes
bathroom: room with a bathtub, but which might not have a toilet
bedsit: efficiency apartment
biscuit: cookie
bill (*in a restaurant*): check
biro: ball-point pen
bog: toilet (slang)
bonnet: hood of a car
boot: trunk of a car
brolly: umbrella
bum-bag: fanny pack (note: "*fanny*" is a coarse term; don't use it)

chemist: pharmacy or pharmacist
chips: french fries
coach: bus travelling between cities
crisps: chips, usually potato
crumpet: English muffin

dress circle: mezzanine seats in a theatre
dustbin: wastebasket or trashcan

first floor: second floor, one above street level
flat: apartment
fortnight: two weeks
full stop (*at the end of a sentence*): period

ground floor: first floor, the one at street level

hire: rent, as in "to hire a taxi"
holiday: vacation

jam: jelly
jelly: Jell-O
jumper: sweater

kitchen roll: paper towels
knickers: women's underpants; short trousers are "plus-fours"
knock up: morning wake-up call

let: rent, as in "to let a flat"
lift: elevator
loo: toilet
lorry: truck

mac (or macintosh): raincoat

nappy: diaper

pants: men's underpants. Say *trousers* instead.
pasty (pronounced "*pass*-tee"): meat and vegetable pie
pavement: sidewalk
petrol: gasoline
plimsolls: tennis shoes
pram: stroller, baby carriage
pudding: dessert

queue: line

return ticket: round-trip ticket
ring up: call (on the telephone)

self-catering: self-contained apartment with kitchen
sellotape: Scotch tape
smart casual: neat but informal dress
sorry: excuse me
stalls: orchestra seats in a theatre
starter: appetizer
stone: 14 pounds
subway: undergound walkway beneath a street
sweet: dessert

ta: thanks (slang)
tick: check off, as "Please tick the appropriate box."
tights: pantyhose
toilet roll: toilet paper
torch: flashlight
trainers: tennis shoes
trunk call: long-distance telephone call
tube: subway

Underground: subway

VAT: Value Added Tax; added to almost everything in Britain

vest: undershirt

w.c.: toilet

Index

Index

Index

Index

Other titles of interest

A Traveller's History of London
by Richard Tames

*". . . recommended for both would-be visitors and armchair travellers
alike: It provides a historical background to London and condenses
2000 years of history into a lively, readable format which will prove
particularly inviting for history buffs who want to have the book in
hand while visiting parks, museums and historical sites around
London."*

—The Midwest Book Review

ISBN 1-56656-109-4 $13.95 pb

A Traveller's History of England
by Christopher Daniell (3rd ed.)

*"This compact volume . . . delivers a solid, comprehensive and
entertaining overview of England's history . . . a delightful source."*

—Library Journal

This book gives a comprehensive and enjoyable survey of England's
past from prehistoric times right through to the present.

ISBN 1-56656-202-3 $14.95 pb

American Walks in London
Ten Step-by-Step Itineraries for North American Visitors
by Richard Tames

The ten walks in this book (each starting and ending at a Tube stop)
will take you to all London's most famous sights as well as to places
you never knew existed—showing them to you as you've never
seen them before.

En route, the author recommends:
• Restaurants, cafés, fast-food and take-out places • Pubs and wine
bars • Public toilets • Delays and diversions • Shopping and souvenirs
• Sights and sites, museums and galleries • Bus and walking tours.

ISBN 1-56656-213-9 $14.95 pb

Interlink's Bestselling Travel Publications

The Traveller's History Series

The Traveller's History series is designed for travellers who want more historical background on the country they are visiting than can be found in a tour guide. Each volume offers a complete and authoritative history of the country from the earliest times up to the present day. A Gazetteer cross-referenced to the main text pinpoints the historical importance of sights and towns.

Illustrated with maps and line drawings, this literate and lively series makes ideal before-you-go reading, and is just as handy tucked into suitcase or backpack.

A Traveller's History of China (2nd ed.)	$14.95 pb
A Traveller's History of England (3rd ed.)	$14.95 pb
A Traveller's History of France (4th ed.)	$12.95 pb
A Traveller's History of Greece (3rd ed.)	$14.95 pb
A Traveller's History of India	$14.95 pb
A Traveller's History of Ireland (3rd ed.)	$14.95 pb
A Traveller's History of Italy (4th ed.)	$14.95 pb
A Traveller's History of Japan (2nd ed.)	$14.95 pb
A Traveller's History of London	$13.95 pb
A Traveller's History of North Africa	$14.95 pb
A Traveller's History of Paris (2nd ed.)	$14.95 pb
A Traveller's History of Russia (3rd ed.)	$14.95 pb
A Traveller's History of Scotland (3rd ed.)	$13.95 pb
A Traveller's History of Spain (3rd ed.)	$14.95 pb
A Traveller's History of Turkey (3rd ed.)	$14.95 pb

The Traveller's Wine Guides

Illustrated with specially commissioned photographs (wine usually seems to be made in attractive surroundings) as well as maps, the books in this series describe the wine-producing regions of each country. The authors recommend itineraries, list wineries, describe the local cuisines, suggest wine bars and restaurants, and provide a mass of practical information—much of which is not readily available elsewhere.

A Traveller's Wine Guide to France	$17.95 pb
A Traveller's Wine Guide to Germany	$17.95 pb
A Traveller's Wine Guide to Italy	$17.95 pb
A Traveller's Wine Guide to Spain	$17.95 pb

The Independent Walker Series

This unique series is designed for visitors who enjoy walking and getting off the beaten track. In addition to their value as general guides, each volume is peerless as a walker's guide, allowing travellers to see all of the great sites, enjoy the incomparable beauty of the countryside, and maintain a high level of physical fitness while travelling through the popular tourist destinations.

Each guide includes:

• Practical information on thirty-five extraordinary short walks (all planned as day hikes and are between 2 and 9 miles), including: how to get there, where to stay, trail distance, walking time, difficulty rating, explicit trail directions and a vivid general description of the trail and local sights.
• Numerous itineraries: The Grand Tour which embraces all thirty-five walks; regional itineraries; and thematic itineraries.
• One planning map for the itineraries and thirty-five detailed trail maps.
• Trail notes broken down into an easy-to-follow checklist format.
• A "Walks-at-a-Glance" section which provides capsule summaries
of all the walks.
• Black and white photographs.
• Before-you-go helpful hints.

The Independent Walker's Guide to France	$14.95 pb
The Independent Walker's Guide to Great Britain	$14.95 pb
The Independent Walker's Guide to Italy	$14.95 pb
The Independent Walker's Guide to Ireland	$14.95 pb

The Spectrum Guides

Each title in the series includes over 200 full-color photographs and provides a comprehensive and detailed description of the country together with all the essential data that tourists, business visitors or students are likely to require.

Spectrum Guide to India	$21.95 pb
Spectrum Guide to Jordan	$21.95 pb
Spectrum Guide to Mauritius	$19.95 pb
Spectrum Guide to Nepal	$21.95 pb
Spectrum Guide to Tanzania	$21.95 pb
Spectrum Guide to Uganda	$19.95 pb
Spectrum Guide to the United Arab Emirates	$21.95 pb

The *In Focus* Guides

This new series of country guides is designed for travellers and students who want to understand the wider picture and build up an overall knowledge of a country. Each *In Focus* guide is a lively and thought-provoking introduction to the country's people, politics and culture.

Brazil in Focus	$12.95 pb
Chile in Focus	$12.95 pb
Costa Rica in Focus	$12.95 pb
The Dominican Republic in Focus	$12.95 pb
Eastern Caribbean in Focus	$12.95 pb
Ecuador in Focus	$12.95 pb
Guatemala in Focus	$12.95 pb
Jamaica in Focus	$12.95 pb
Peru in Focus	$12.95 pb

Available at good bookstores everywhere.
We encourage you to support your local bookseller.

To order or request our complete catalog,
please call us at **1-800-238-LINK** or write to:
Interlink Publishing
46 Crosby Street, Northampton, MA 01060